When You're Up to Your Eyeballs in Alligators

LARRY WILDE

Books by Larry Wilde

Hardcover

The Larry Wilde Treasury of Laughter
The Larry Wilde Library of Laughter
The Complete Book of Ethnic Humor
How the Great Comedy Writers Create Laughter
The Great Comedians Talk About Comedy

Paperback

You're Never Too Old To Laugh
The Dumb, Dumber, Dumbest Joke Book
The Official Golf Lovers Joke Book
The Merriest Book of Christmas Humor
The Official Locker Room Joke Book
The Ultimate Pet Lovers Joke Book
The Ultimate Book of Ethnic Humor
The Official Computer Freaks Joke Book
    (with Steve Wozniak)
The Official WASP Joke Book
The Official All America Joke Book
The Ultimate Lawyers Joke Book
More The Official Doctors Joke Book
The Official Executives Joke Book
The Official Sports Maniacs Joke Book
The Official Politicians Joke Book
The Official Rednecks Joke Book
The *Last* Official Smart Kids Joke Book
The Larry Wilde Book of Limericks
The Official Lawyers Joke Book
The Official Doctors Joke Book
More The Official Smart Kids/Dumb Parents Joke Book
The Official Book of Sick Jokes
The Official Cat Lovers/Dog Lovers Joke Book
The Official Golfers Joke Book
The Official Smart Kids/Dumb Parents Joke Book
The Official Religious/Not So Religious Joke Book

**34 additional titles published by Pinnacle
and Bantam Books wherever books are sold.**

When You're Up to Your Eyeballs in Alligators

LARRY WILDE

Jester Press
Carmel
California

Library of Congress Cataloging-in-Publication Data

Wilde, Larry
  when you're up to your eyeballs in alligators/ Larry Wilde
  p.   cm.
    1. Wit and humor--History and criticism. 2. Laughter
            3. American wit and humor. I. Title
        PN6147.W55 1997 809.7 -- dc21 CIP 97-22849
              Preassigned LCCN: 97-93852

        ISBN 0-945040-02-4 (hardcover) $30.00
        Includes bibliographical references.

    Jester Press books are available at special
  discounts for bulk purchases, for sales promotions,
    premiums, fund raising or educational use.
          For details contact:

            Jester Press
        25470 Cañada Drive
        Carmel, CA 93923-8926

iv

> "What makes life
> worth living?
> To be born with
> the gift of laughter.
> And a sense that
> the world is mad."
>
> — Rafael Sabatini,
> author, *Scaramouche*

Dedication

To the funny men and woman
who have helped to replace pain and sorrow
with fun and laughter.

And the scientists, sociologists, journalists,
psychologists, researchers, academics
and health care practitioners
who have made humor a household word.

Acknowledgments

To my friends,
Nancy Baker Jacobs, Jerry Jacobs,
Layne Littlepage, Jeffrey Evans,
Autumn Fuentes,
my agent, Jane Jordan Browne,
and to my editor, best friend,
travel companion, lover,
comforter, advisor
and beautiful spouse
Her Majesty Maryruth .

Contents

ix

Laughter: The Splendid Spirit Lifter
Humor: The Miraculous Mood Elevator
Sick Humor Syndrome   A Good Sense of Humor Lasts
Humor Breaks the Ice and Smoothes Communication
Laughing Your Alligators in the Face

A Short Primer in the Nuts and Bolts of Comedy
5 Reasons Why Presenters Rely on Humor
Anecdotes   One-liners   Jokes   Funny Stories
Riddles   Puns   Limericks

You Can Learn How to be Funnier   Memorizing the
Punch Line First   Mince Words   Rehearse Repeat Rehearse
Don't Laugh at Your Own Jokes
Don't Blame the Audience if it Doesn't Respond
Personalizing Your Humor
Make Sure The Audience Understands Every Word
Note to the Pros: Using Quotes
Experimenting to Achieve Desired Effect
Failure to Prepare is Preparation for Failure

Introduction

"Humor is
like a
bulletproof vest
that protects
you against
negative emotions."

—NORMAN COUSINS,
author

A sense of humor
is having the ability
to find the absurd
in the ordinary.

Introduction

White House insiders acknowledge that while Lyndon Johnson was president he had a slogan in the oval office that read:

When you're up to your ass in alligators
it's difficult to remind yourself
that your initial objective
was to drain the swamp.

Times have changed.
The swamp is much deeper now. Most of us are up to our eyeballs. So before we get in over our

heads we need to stop, take a breather and put it all in perspective.

How do we do that?

People who are most successful at this exhilarating game we call life have discovered an invaluable secret: *They take their work seriously but not themselves.*

In doing so, part of their success lies in their ability to achieve balance. They seem to have incorporated in their makeup an ingredient that has a positive effect on the people around them: an infectious sense of humor.

When one develops a joyful attitude, a way of looking at life light-heartedly, anything is possible.

When You're Up To Your Eyeballs in Alligators offers a prescription for dealing with everyday difficulties.

> ## "The No. 1 sin in life is taking yourself too seriously."
>
> —TOM PETERS, author, management consultant

Between these covers you'll see how some of the most preeminent people in history have added pleasure, productivity, even years to life just by developing an appreciation for one of our greatest natural resources — the gift of laughter.

Is it possible that laughing out loud could be more beneficial to our overall health than anyone ever imagined?

Why is it essential for humans to nurture a sense of fun and play all through their lives?

Is there a demonstrable connection between humor and well-being?

These are questions I began considering more than thirty years ago. Thanks to scientific research, proven theories and anecdotal evidence the answers have finally surfaced.

In the following pages you'll discover, as I have, the magical, mysterious, startling, wonderful secrets about humor.

- How humor can improve physical and mental health, increase longevity, and put more meaning into life.

- Why humor is vital to achieve balance and perspective.

- Why "lightening up" is essential to survive and thrive in difficult and changing times.

- Why humor is an important strategy for stimulating a creative, exuberant work environment.

And to enhance your humor appreciation.

- How various forms of humor are used to evoke laughter, and how they are easily incorporated into our lives.

> "Humor is a great thing,
> the saving thing, after all.
> The minute it crops up,
> all our hardnesses yield,
> all our irritations and
> resentments flit away,
> and a sunny spirit
> takes their place."
>
> — MARK TWAIN,
> author

THE BEGINNING

During the height of World War II, a scrawny, big nosed teenager stood on the stage of Lincoln High School facing a general assembly of 1200 students. He was the closing act in a talent show being presented by the senior class.

The boy had slicked his hair down over the right eye and held a black pocket comb above his lips. He began screaming unintelligible, guttural sounds with a German accent. Posturing, mugging, pounding a fist into the palm of his hand.

The audience laughed uproariously.

For a finish, he extended his right arm in the Nazi salute, shouted, "Heil Hitler!" and then stuck out his tongue and blew a "raspberry."

Wild laughter filled the school auditorium.

That comic imitation of the great dictator was my first appearance in front of a large crowd, my initiation into the addicting, wondrous world of humor.

The laughter that day permeated my soul and motivated me to spend a lifetime performing, writing, studying, teaching, researching, analyzing, and advocating humor.

All through school I'd made classmates laugh. I'd learned as a boy that making bullies laugh was a way to wiggle out of a beating.

As the only Jewish kid in a poor Irish/Black neighborhood I realized that they couldn't call me "Jew boy," or "Heinie" or give me a black eye or fat lip if they were laughing. I wormed my way into their affections by tickling their funny bones.

What they never knew was that I loved their laughter more than they did. Making an ass of myself and being rewarded with the soothing, exhilarating, approving sound of laughter proved irresistible.

Years later I joked about growing up in the toughest part of the city:

Mine was a tough neighborhood. If you didn't get home by ten, you were declared legally dead.

I went back there recently. They were so thrilled to see me, they staged a holdup in my honor.

I just heard that the city is planning to tear down my old neighborhood and improve it by putting up a slum.

During two years in the Marine Corps, I became the first non-com comedian. I figured if I could make the hoodlums in my old neighborhood laugh, leathernecks would be a pushover.

So I put on shows for Marines at Camp Lejeune, North Carolina. (Hey, it beats marching, jujitsu and schlepping.)

At the University of Miami in Florida, I parlayed my reputation as "campus comic" from appearing in school shows to earning real bread making the tourists laugh at Miami Beach hotels.

I was hooked on comedy.

I went from a kid who didn't crack a book in high school — I graduated 170th in a class of 172 — to a college student who read everything from the Greek comedies to the plays of Oscar Wilde and George Bernard Shaw.

My appetite was whetted and I poured over the best humor writers I could get my hands on.

8

Everyone from Mark Twain and Robert Benchley to James Thurber and P.G. Wodehouse.

I became a humorholic.

> ## "A sense of humor is a sense of proportion."
>
> —KAHLIL GIBRAN,
> author

COMEDY CAREER vs SENSE OF HUMOR

After becoming a professional comedian I discovered that there's a vast chasm between being a comedy performer and simply loving humor.

There are many comedians who are notoriously sour human beings. Their lives begin and end with performing. Off stage, they are sad and bitter and don't really have a sense of humor about themselves.

They know how to make others laugh, writing the joke, delivering it, timing it. They can put a brilliant routine together. They can promote themselves and even be wildly successful. They are very serious about their work. But like so many other driven individuals they fail to nurture a playful spirit in their personal lives.

The ingredients for a healthy sense of humor are not much different than the essentials for a happy life. All it takes is the following:

- An optimistic point of view.

- A positive outlook.

- The ability to see the absurdities of life.

- A flexibility of attitude and intellect.

- A balanced perspective.

- The desire to surrender to one's playful nature.

- The willingness to forgive yourself and others.

> "I have seen
> what a laugh
> can do.
> It can transform
> almost unbearable
> tears into
> something bearable,
> even hopeful."
>
> — BOB HOPE,
> comedian

POWER OF HUMOR

What has a lifetime steeped in all aspects of humor taught me?

1. Humor is one of the most powerful of human forces.

The ability to laugh counter-balances the human capacity for destroying our planet. And it's up to all of us to see that joy and laughter are never outweighed by tragedy.

2. Humor can bring opposing sides together.

Robert Reich, the 4-foot-11-inch former Democratic Secretary of Labor in the Clinton administration and Alan J. Simpson, the 6-foot-5-inch retired conservative Wyoming Republican Senator were both teaching classes at Harvard University.

They had been long-time close friends and were being interviewed side-by-side on C-Span.

"You've asked us a lot of questions," said Simpson to the interviewer, "but there's one that's been on your mind that you might've been afraid to ask so I'll ask it for you:

"How could two men, a big tall fella and a small little guy, with opposite political views, know each other so many years and be such good friends?

"Well, I'll tell you: Humor. We make each other laugh."

"If I had no
sense of humor,
I should long ago
have committed suicide."

—MAHATMA GANDHI,
spiritual leader

3. Humor breaks the ice, and smoothes communication.

The students in my Humor Appreciation class at UCLA came from every walk of life. Among them were college kids, hopeful comedians, Ph.D's, medical doctors, lawyers, teachers, business executives, seniors and homemakers. At a fall semester the class included a woman who had recently immigrated from China.

As always I asked participants their reasons for taking the class. The answers varied. Two teachers wanted to become comedy writers. A doctor admitted he was trying to develop a better bedside manner. One trial lawyer wanted to become more relaxed in front of juries.

When I asked the Chinese woman, she stood and replied in her broken English, "I like find out more about American. What make them laugh. Then I know how to be happy with them."

The whole class applauded.

4. Humor stimulates the free-flow of creative juices.

At BookExpo America, Art Buchwald was autographing his latest. I'd always been a big fan of his work and when I interviewed him for *How The Great Comedy Writers Create Laughter*, we became friends.

"I was thinking about you just this morning," he said, as we shook hands. "I had to get my column written so I began reading one of your joke books. It starts me thinking funny."

"This I conceive
to be the chemical
function of humor:
to change the
character
of our thought."

— LIN YOUTANG

5. **Humor strengthens the bonds of relationships among parents, children, husbands, wives, lovers, friends, colleagues and co-workers**

A grey-haired woman and her pretty ten-year-old granddaughter, Jennifer, were our dining room seat mates on an Alaskan cruise. Grandma Carolee related the good humor practiced by her family by recountng this incident:

One afternoon she was napping on the living room sofa when little Jennifer — six, at the time — awakened her by running her fingers across Grandma's face.

"What are you doing?" asked the grandmother.

"Daddy, told me you can tell the age of a tree by counting the lines," said little Jennifer. "I'm trying to figure out how old you are."

6. **Humor is the glue that cements coopera-tion, loyalty and teamwork on the job.**

The CEO of a large publishing house noticed that the marketing staff at the weekly meeting was quite nervous. He was informed by his secretary that somehow the latest sales figures hadn't arrived in time for appraisal.

He began the meeting by saying, "Just think, if Moses were alive today, God could have faxed the Ten Commandments to him."

They laughed.

It broke the tension.

7. Humor — quick, fast, reliable and effective — is a wonder drug for stress, the best remedy we have against emotional burnout.

The personnel director for a large steel company arrived home after a long stressful, pressure packed day at the office.

He was able to let off steam by saying to his wife, "What a bright world this would be if all new employees were only half as good as their resumes said they would be."

8. Humor is a miraculous healer of mind and body.

Humor breathes life back into the human spirit. It gives us a rich, central core of humanity full of wisdom and insight. It has the power to take the sting out of the alligator bites and provides us with a life raft of balance and sanity to get us safely through the swamps we all must face.

> "If you're not
> allowed to
> laugh in heaven,
> I don't want
> to go there."
>
> — MARTIN LUTHER (1483-1546)

THE WONDER DRUG

There are many ways to become rich. Libraries are filled with volumes on how to achieve wealth. But like everything in life we must be willing to pay the price.

Nobody escapes. Worry warts, workaholics, and perfectionists, in our driving desire to achieve, often compromise our health, our marriages and family relationships.

Laughter is a timeless wonder drug. It's a tension-relieving medicine that permits people to cope with pressure. Indeed, our lives would be cold and colorless indeed without humor or what playwright Moss Hart called, "refreshment of the spirit."

Many of us couldn't get through the day without our Vitamin L (for laughs provided by Molly Ivins, Dave Barry, Art Buchwald, or Russell Baker.)

Life without the works of Woody Allen, Neil Simon, Mel Brooks, Billy Crystal, and Robin Williams?

No thanks.

And who could give up the cartoon strips of Bill Waterson, Charles Schultz and Garry Trudeau?

Readers Digest recognized the value of humor in their regular feature, *Laughter Is The Best Medicine,* which is partly responsible for the magazine's long run. It's a feature that many readers turned to first, just as cartoon fans skim *The New Yorker.*

Little wonder the bible declares

> A *merry heart doeth good*
> *like a medicine.*

Naysayers and negative thinkers, the gloomy and depressed, the somber and sour faced, continue to belittle the benefits of indulging in fun and laughter.

What's all the fuss over cheerfulness?

Humor doesn't cost anything. How can it possibly be so valuable?

In this book you'll discover the latest scientific studies and research data underscored by personal experiences. Once and for all, the skeptics will be satisfied by knowing that

- Humor provides a socially acceptable release for anxiety, fear, embarrassment, anger, hostility, depression and frustration.

- Humor promotes understanding and is a great way to build inter-personal relationships.

- Humor smoothes communication in business and is unparalleled in forging a sense of trust and cooperation.

- Humor makes it easy to retain facts and information.

- Humor in health care is essential for opening communication, boosting morale and supporting the body's natural healing powers.

The growing appreciation for the therapeutic value of laughter didn't just happened overnight. Over 400 years ago, the English writer and clergyman Robert Burton noted that "Humor purges the blood, making the body young, lively, and fit for any manner of employment."

Americans have become more aware of humor and its benefits in recent years due to both the research on the subject and the proliferation of comedy clubs and TV shows.

Down through the centuries kings relied on court jesters to provide merriment for the royal family and members of the court.

Greek tragedies always included funny characters for comic relief. The theatrical tradition of comedy continued into vaudeville where characters stepped out from behind the roles they portrayed, created their own personae and talked directly to the audience. Thus giving birth to the stand-up comedian as we know it today.

> **"What soap is to the body, laughter is to the soul."**
>
> — YIDDISH PROVERB

> "We don't laugh
> because we're happy,
> we're happy
> because we laugh."
>
> —WILLIAM JAMES,
> philosopher

IT ONLY HURTS WHEN I DON'T LAUGH

Exactly why laughing makes us feel so good has been the subject of much exploration. Researchers have found significant changes in the levels of stress hormones and increased immune system function when people laugh, which is why laughter is now prescribed for better health.

"We have exercise prescriptions; we have medicine prescriptions — this is a humor prescription," says Lee Berk, assistant research professor of pathology and laboratory medicine at Loma Linda University Schools of Medicine and Public Health.

Berk and his partner, Dr. Stanley Tan, have been studying the physiological effects of "mirthful laughter" since Norman Cousins first helped fund their research in 1983.

Berk and Tan have found that while "negative stress" increases the secretion of stress hormones, "positive stress" — such as laughter — produces changes in the levels of those hormones.

So consciously remembering to look for laughter may be good medical advice.

As we shall see, a good sense of humor is like a first aid kit for dealing with the tensions of our times.

For years humor has been taken for granted. But now some major questions about the critical role it plays in our lives have been answered.

How does the sense of humor we possess influence the quality of our lives?

Is it vital to understand and appreciate the therapeutic value of a humorous outlook?

How can we go about living life with a lighter touch?

No one is foolish enough to say that the changes and the challenges of these times are easy. But we now know that humor may be our most important ally.

When times are tough, when things aren't going the way we want them to, when we're up to our eyeballs in alligators, that's when the benefits of humor become obvious.

When we face up to our responsibilities with a good sense of humor, not even a swamp full of alligators will drag us down.

Laughter is a natural pressure valve. It eases stress, relieves tension. Besides, it's salt free, low calorie, polyunsaturated, it doesn't cost a dime, and as of this printing, it is still tax free.

> **"And if I laugh**
> **at any mortal thing**
> **'Tis that I**
> **may not weep."**
>
> —LORD BYRON,
> poet

A Sense of Humor
— EDGAR A. GUEST

"What shall I give him now?" said God.
"He has the strength with which to plod
The ways of life, the love of right,
The gift of song when the skies are bright.

"Wisdom is planted in his mind,
This man shall be both true and kind,
Earth's beauty shall delight his eyes
And to its glories he shall rise.

"He shall know right from wrong; and he
Defender of the faith shall be;
What more on him can I bestow
Before to earth I let him go?"

Then spake an angel standing near:
"Wisdom is not enough, I fear,
Master, for all that he must do—
Grant him a sense of humor, too.

"Grant him to smile at petty wrong,
The changing moods which sway the throng;
When cares annoy him, show him then
How laughable are angry men!"

Years after, when his strength was tasked,
"What keeps you patient?" he was asked,
"What keeps you brave who are so tried?"
"My sense of humor," he replied.

PROVING THE PERCEPTION

Getting individuals to acknowledge the unconventional premise that a merry mind-set leads to a richer, more healthful, happier life is not simple.

What you will read here comes from my lifetime love affair with humor.

As you've already read, these insights are authenticated by the latest medical research, confirmed and verified by dignitaries, celebrities, world leaders and high achievers in every field.

It all boils down to this — the more humor you put into your life, the better your physical and mental health will be, the more successful you'll become and the longer you'll live.

And here's the best part. Developing a better sense of humor doesn't take any special talent or ability and there's practically no effort.

I'll share with you some very specific strategies, things you can start doing today, that'll help you respond to life more gracefully.

As you incorporate these ideas into your life you'll begin to create a more peaceful and loving you.

After a lifetime in the humor business, observing what makes people laugh and why, I've come to this conclusion: There are five basic steps to how laughter can help us deal with life when we're up to our eyeballs in alligators.

And here they are!

"Happy is the
the person who
— even without money —
keeps their humor."

— GERMAN SAYING

Step One

Rattle
The Rafters

"It's very bad
to suppress laughter.
It goes back
down and spreads
to your hips."

— FRED ALLEN,
comedian

*Even if there is
nothing to laugh about,
laugh on credit.*

You Can Improve
Your Health by Simply
Laughing Out Loud

WE ALL NEED TO BE REMINDED OF THE
importance of laughing out loud. Many of us have
forgotten to appreciate the positive, therapeutic and
healthful benefits that come from the spontaneous
pleasure of laughing.

We get so caught up in our daily obligations it's
very difficult to let ourselves go.

Every day in the workplace, visiting with friends
or family, or just being on a crowded bus, we hear
or see something that's amusing. We know that it's
funny but instead of opening up and expressing the
joy, we keep it bottled up inside.

SUPPRESSING SNICKERS

Often we forget to laugh out loud, to allow ourselves the joy of "getting the giggles" like we did in childhood. Back then, adults were always telling us to "pipe down," "shush," "stifle it," and "cut the comedy" in order to stifle our laughter.

As grownups it seems childish or foolish to many of us to lose ourselves completely in helpless laughter.

But to experience happiness we must nurture a playful spirit with positive thoughts as well as a heavy helping of fun and good cheer. Suppressing laughter is not only unnatural, it may be unhealthful.

What happens when we get into a routine of curbing our laughter? We smile or snicker, or merely nod our heads to acknowledge an amusing anecdote or quip. Too adult and too judgmental to give ourselves over to a good giggle.

After extensive research on the subject Dr. Raymond A. Moody, Jr. reports: "People's natural laughter gets sealed over by inhibition. From early youth they get messages like, 'Don't laugh in church,' 'Don't laugh in school,' or 'Don't laugh in the movies,' etc.

"Pretty soon people become inhibited, they won't open up, and they begin to feel guilty about laughing."

TRICKS OF THE TV TRADE

Another reason people have forgotten how to laugh out loud is because canned laughter on television does it for them.

Recent studies show that TV may be the single biggest cause for lack of reaction and interaction. Most viewers search the channels for entertainment and relaxation. Countless sitcoms attempt to provide that diversion.

Sitcom producers believe viewers, in the privacy of their homes, need prompting to recognize how funny the show is. That audiences require visual or audible stimulus to make them feel comfortable and to hold their attention.

Most sitcom episodes are recorded in a television studio before a live audience. Sometimes when the crowd doesn't react exactly the way the director and producer thinks it should, laughter is dubbed onto the edited film.

They hope by dubbing in the laugh track of a large crowd that it will subliminally prompt the at home viewer to laugh.

But perhaps the theory and practice of dubbing laughs has backfired. After years of being subjected to the sound of canned laughter many television viewers now react silently (if at all) to the supposedly humorous situations. A silent smile or grin. They have gotten out of the habit of laughing out loud — letting themselves go.

THE COUSINS CONNECTION

What's so important about being able to rattle the rafters with our laughter?

Several years ago a breakthrough in the understanding of humor's effect on health came to light. The medical profession was suddenly made aware of something humor devotees have known for ages: Laughter is therapeutic. And it can be a healing factor.

> "I see humor as food. I don't think that the only time people should eat food is when they're ill. An adequate share of humor and laughter represent an essential part of the diet of the healthy person."
>
> — NORMAN COUSINS, author

The catalyst for this astonishing new approach was Norman Cousins, author, lecturer and former editor of the celebrated literary journal, *Saturday Review.*

One man's journey of healing and self-discovery opened the door to a new approach for treating illness.

Laughter was a major factor in Cousins' remarkable recovery from his ailment, a collagen disorder that caused progressive disintegration of the connective tissues in his spine and joints. The illness began when he returned from an emotionally and physically draining trip to the Soviet Union.

Cousins never dreamed that his own methods to cure himself of a life threatening disease would open the floodgates of scientific research and forever change the thinking of the medical community on the kinship between health and humor.

In reconstructing the causes for his illness, Cousins determined that adrenal exhaustion was a likely factor. He reasoned that "if negative forces like tension and stress could weaken the body to the point where it could succumb to germs, then positive forces — confidence, joy, faith, hope, love, laughter and the will to live — might have the opposite effect."

With the support of his doctor, Cousins devised his own treatment program which included large doses of laughter. He watched clips from the classic television series, *Candid Camera*, as well as old Marx Brothers movies, and he read the funniest writers he could find.

The results were startling. He found that ten minutes of belly laughs produced an anesthetic effect which allowed him at least two hours of pain-free sleep. Sedimentation rates taken before and after laugher exercises provided quantifiable evidence that laughter is indeed good medicine.

When Cousins first reported his findings in the *New England Journal of Medicine* the article prompted more than 3000 letters from doctors supporting his ideas and contributing accounts of similar experiences.

Almost overnight the posture toward humor and its salutary benefits became the subject of surveys, studies, research and writings. Health care professionals soon formally recognized what the *Readers Digest* had been proclaiming for decades. *Laughter Is The Best Medicine.*

> "Genuine laughter
> is a vent of the soul,
> the nostrils of
> the heart,
> and it is just
> as necessary for
> health and happiness
> as spring water is
> for a trout."
>
> —JOSH BILLINGS,
> humorist

MIRACLE OF MIRTH

Now, after years of research, there is evidence that the physical act of laughing is more beneficial to our health than anybody ever imagined.

Laughing out loud causes the body to release natural painkillers as well as antibodies that fight off infection. The chemicals are endorphins, the same released fluids that helped Norman Cousins live through part of each day without pain.

Laughing out loud oxygenates the blood, which in turn stimulates circulation, which in turn massages the vital organs.

LAUGHTER AND SEX

Does laughing out loud improve your sex life?

The jury is still out on this one. But there is something that is known for sure, it definitely keeps your partner awake a little longer.

On the subject of sex and laughter, comedian Will Durst says, "It's okay to laugh in the bedroom as long as you don't point."

Dr. Ruth Westheimer, the celebrated countess of courtship, adds another practical piece of advice, "Some tickling or telling funny stories in bed can make sex more interesting."

HAVING FUN: WHO NEEDS IT?

There are those who believe that laughter, play and having fun are a waste of time. Even a sin.

Take my father.

One Sunday when my brothers, sister and I were kids, my father took us to Coney Island — the poor man's Riviera. Coney Island was famous for its beach, boardwalk and hundreds of food stands selling hot dogs, hamburgers, corn on the cob, cotton candy, ice cream, frozen custard and other delectable delights created especially for a child's discriminating taste buds. But most of all, crowds flocked to Coney Island because there was a roller coaster, motor scooters, a merry-go-round, Ferris wheel and other assorted rides.

> **"Cultivating your sense of playfulness is the key to learning to lighten up in the midst of stress."**
>
> — PAUL McGHEE, PhD.

As we piled out of his 1932 Buick, my father gathered us together and his words have remained forever stamped in my memory. "Okay," he announced, "you can have frankfurters and corn on the cob and frozen custard but don't ask for no money to go on those rides."

For an Austrian immigrant who landed on Ellis Island as a teenager, my father couldn't conceive of spending difficult-to-come-by cash at the height of the depression on anything as superficial as the merry-go-round.

He worked endless hours to save enough to transport his sister, brother and mother from Europe. Then he married and was soon blessed with four kids to raise. Playing or having fun was not an activity he knew. In his mind, there was no room for play. Spending money to ride a merry-go-round just for fun was squandering hard-earned cash. The word "fun" did not exist in his vocabulary.

Many poor immigrants like my father were born to and grew up in a work ethic that did not include the appreciation of anything frivolous. Celebrations were limited to weddings, births and confirmations.

In our household, not even birthdays were observed. I was thirty-years-old before my first birthday party. I invited friends and threw a party for myself.

Today, we now recognize the importance of holidays, vacations and having fun. Medical research has helped us to understand that the healthiest human beings are those who have learned to balance work and play.

Unfortunately many of us still have not got the message. Louis Harris & Associates and Interep Research Division reports that over the past twenty years, Americans have increased the number of hours spent at work, while cutting back on time devoted to leisure pursuits.

And this workaholism is spreading globally. In a British television documentary on life in the former Soviet Union, it was reported that Russian kids are now being taught in school how to play. With both parents working long hours scrambling to put bread on the table, many children have not learned to indulge in fun activities or how to interact with other children in the play that is so vital to their development.

"Nobody says
you must laugh,
but a sense of humor
can help you overlook
the unattractive,
tolerate the unpleasant,
cope with
the unexpected,
and smile
through the day."

— ANN LANDERS,
columnist

WELL BEING DEPENDS ON LEVITY

An every day playful spirit enhances emotional and physical health.

O. Carl Simonton, the noted California physician and best-selling author who specializes in cancer treatment, reveals why he incorporates humor into patient care. He says, "the very latest research has discovered that laughing stimulates chemicals that reduce, inhibit and suppress the production of cancer cells and can cut back the illness of tumors."

We can learn to calm ourselves so that our bodies can produce these chemicals. And one of the ways to calm ourselves is by laughter.

Medical science has pills to lower blood pressure, drugs to fight the flu and medicines to overcome miscarriages, but laughing is a cure that doesn't need to be produced by a pharmaceutical company.

Anatomy of an Illness, by Norman Cousins, a book I highly recommend, contains my favorite Cousins quote, "Laughter is internal jogging."

Who would've ever imagined that the fun of laughing could generate so many happy and healthful benefits?

Of course, when we laugh we feel happy. And research indicates that happy people are healthier and tend to live longer.

Some doctors now say that cheerful people resist disease better than grumpy ones.

The surly bird catches the germ.*

*More pun fun in Humor 101.

"Cancer is probably
the most unfunny
thing in the world,
but I'm a comedian,
and even cancer
couldn't stop me
from seeing humor in
what I went through."

— GILDA RADNER,
comedian

LAUGHTER ENHANCES IMMUNITY

Norman Cousins often felt misunderstood about the power of laughter. He believed what made the difference for him was the sense of empowerment he derived from being an active participant in his treatment.

Although he used funny films to induce positive emotions, he always emphasized hope, a sense of control and loving support as critical factors in healing. Still, follow-up research supports his theory that laughter has a powerful and positive effect on immunity.

On the PBS documentary, *Healing and the Mind* hosted by Bill Moyers, evidence was presented that indicated there are physical and chemical links between the mind and the immune system. Simply put, emotional stress may compromise the body's ability to fight off disease.

There is evidence suggesting that laughter can significantly ease stress and thereby bolster resistance. Researchers from Western New England College monitored immune-boosting chemicals in two groups of students. One group watched humorous video tapes, the other a serious movie. In the students who watched the funny films, the concentration of immune-boosting chemicals rose while those who watched the serious film showed no change.

Dr. Arnold Fox, the renowned Los Angeles internist, states in his book, *Immune for Life*, "Your thoughts change your biochemistry and your biochemistry affects your health and happiness. So it behooves us to keep our thoughts as happy and as positive as we can."

"Happiness is the key to a long life," reports Dr. George E. Vaillant in a salubrious *Spring Magazine* article. "People who suffer from anxiety and depression often age quickly and die prematurely. This has a much greater effect on longevity than being overweight, smoking or drinking."

Still another secret to well-being comes with the capacity to laugh at life's challenges. Laughing out loud releases tension, aids digestion and restores the body's chemical balance.

This strategy can be especially invaluable for members of the medical profession.

Clifford C. Kuhn, Professor of Psychiatry and Medical Director University of Louisville School of Medicine has been assisting comedian Jerry Lewis in humor lectures. Lewis speaks at medical centers, university clinics, and hospitals, pointing out the need for doctors, nurses and others in healthcare to recognize the value of a sense of humor in order to counterbalance their stress from dealing with pain and suffering.

Lewis and Dr. Kuhn have formed a strong bond in their continuing effort to encourage and enlighten healthcare professionals about the benefits of humor. Through his experiences with Jerry Lewis and years of study on the subject, Dr. Kuhn offers these views: "Laughter is a potent reliever of stress, a stimulant to the immune system, an effective analgesic, a stabilizer of mood, a resource for problem solving, creativity and productivity, and a pleasant enhancer of communication, collaboration and morale."

Study after study indicates that laughter is every bit as important to our overall health as a proper diet and exercise.

"I don't know
anyone
who knows
how to laugh,
who has
constipation."

— NORMAN COUSINS,
author.

LAUGHTER: THERAPY FOR GRIEF

I had just finished speaking at a luncheon and was heading for my car in the parking lot when a middle-aged woman stopped me.

She was smiling broadly but I couldn't help notice that her eyes were red, the mascara smeared and her face flushed. "I really wasn't up to coming to this meeting," she said. "My husband passed away suddenly six months ago and I've been having a rough time."

"This was the first day I've laughed out loud and it felt great. It broke the tension and sorrow I had been cemented in. Your message helped me put my grief into perspective. I'm finally realizing that I need to go on with my life. If nothing else, I can laugh, and that tells me I can make it."

"Humor is
a means of
obtaining pleasure
in spite of the
distressing effects
that interface with it."

— SIGMUND FREUD,
psychiatrist

LAUGHTER EASES TRAUMA

Just before taking off on my United Airlines flight to New York, a friendly voice came over the loud speaker. It was First Flight Attendant Jan Brown-Lohr doing her usual preliminary monologue — pointing out the emergency exits, how to fasten seat belts, use the floating seat cushions and oxygen mask and stressing the no smoking regulations. In short, the same old announcements we've all heard on a hundred occasions, but this time they sounded very special. Jan presented them in an amusing way and made the passengers laugh.

She told me later, "I realized people were tuning out. They had heard all about safety features on a plane. I thought if it was presented in a little different manner — in a humorous way — I would make a deeper impression, even relax them."

Several years before, on July 19, 1989 a United DC-10 jetliner en route from Denver to Chicago crashed into an Iowa cornfield. 111 persons died.

Jan Brown-Lohr was one of the 185 people who survived. "Laughter helped us heal and benefited our well-being," she told me. "My parish priest said God has a sense of humor. So if he does I think we better follow suit.

"After the crash — having landed upside down, the plane was on fire. One of the passengers had a large blood-stained hole in his shirt. It was as if the shirt had been through a shredder. He looked down at the shirt, then up at me and said, "I don't think my wife is gonna be able to launder this.' I laughed and thought, 'Now there's a sense of humor.'"

*Jan Brown-Lohr has been honored by The Association of Flight Attendants as well as *Conde Nast Traveler* for her untiring efforts to mandate child-restraint seats on aircraft.

"If you don't
have wrinkles,
you haven't
laughed enough."

— PHYLLIS DILLER,
comedian

LAUGH AND LOSE WEIGHT?

Every time we laugh out loud — a good solid belly laugh — we use up 35 calories.

Think of that the next time you're stymied over which video to rent. A good comedy might help burn off that bucket o'popcorn.

There have been dozens of diet crazes over the years. You've heard their claims:

"Lose 8 pounds a week."
"Get rid of 10 pounds a day."
"Burn off 20 pounds a minute."
"Why count calories?"
"Eat a dozen grapefruit."
"Drink 30 quarts of water."
"Buy the book."
"Get the pills."
"Take the shots."

Three months later you're right back where you started. The best remedy may be laughter.

If nothing else, diets are fertile ground for comedy. A friend of mine once announced that he was on a sea food diet. I said, "What's that?" He said, "Every food I see, I eat."

And during lunch at a New Orleans restaurant I overheard two businessmen:

"Seems to me you're getting a little slimmer," said one.
"I should be," replied the other. "I'm on a high protein diet. Nothing but the finest prime steaks and chops. And would you believe it? In just one week I've lost a hundred and eighteen dollars!"

Then there's the Prozac Diet. You don't lose any weight but you don't care.

And the Garlic Diet. You don't lose any weight but you look smaller from a distance.

Forget them all!

The quickest, easiest, least expensive, most delightful way to lose weight ever created: Larry's Vitamin "L" Diet.

Exercise your funny bone!

No special equipment.

No pills.

No hundred dollar shoes.

Laugh 15 times a day — the minimum daily requirement — and you burn 525 calories.

Yes, folks! You can laugh your ass off!

Of all the healthful benefits offered by rattling the rafters, dieting by laughing could become a trend.

The first diet ever conceived where you can lose weight and have fun at the same time.

> ## "Laughter... the most civilized music in the world."
>
> **— PETER USTINOV,**
> actor

LAUGHTER DIFFUSES TYPE A BEHAVIOR

When we become overly emotional about our jobs and take ourselves too seriously we are likely to suffer burnout. Especially those of us in pressure-packed, high-stress professions.

Dr. Meyer Friedman, the renowned cardiologist who co-developed with Dr. Ray H. Rosenman the concept of Type A behavior, runs an institute bearing his name at Mount Zion Medical Center in San Francisco.

Dr. Friedman has been helping patients who have suffered massive coronaries overcome the risk of future heart attacks. He prescribes living a more relaxed, easy-going lifestyle in which humor plays a significant role.

Dr. Friedman's years of research in heart disease have led him to conclude, "The person most effectively protecting himself against the continued progress of coronary artery disease is the person willing to see himself and his affairs as ludicrously unimportant in the planetary scheme of things."

A colleague of Dr. Friedman's tells this story to the delight of his patients:

> *A doctor completed an examination of his Type A patient and said, "I'm sorry to have to tell you this, but you need a heart transplant. It's very serious, very costly."*
>
> *"How much are we talkin' about?" asked the patient.*
>
> *"Well," said the M.D., "I've got a little heart in the freezer that belonged to a 35 year-old fellow. He smoked a little, drank a little and had very high*

cholesterol. It will cost you a hundred thousand dollars."

"What else have you got?"

"We have the heart of a 20-year-old decathlon runner who never smoked or drank. He was in perfect physical condition. That one is two hundred thousand."

"Doc, I'm only gonna do this once, what's the best thing you got?"

"If you really want to go first class, we've got the heart of a 65-year-old fellow. The guy smoked three packs of cigarettes every day, drank two quarts of whiskey, never exercised and had high cholesterol. It'll cost you one million dollars."

"Wow! Why does this one cost so much more than all the others?"

"Well, this is the heart of an attorney and it's never been used."

> **"Humor is contagious. Laughter is infectious. Both are good for your health."**
>
> — WILLIAM FRY, JR. M.D.

If you have trouble letting yourself go, but recognize the benefits of laughing till you rattle the rafters and you do it, eventually it will become second nature.

Psychotherapist Annette Goodheart offers this suggestion: "If you can't laugh spontaneously — fake it till you make it."

Dr. Friedman in his book, *Treating Type A Behavior and Your Heart*, recommends another tip for a long healthy life. Learn to laugh at yourself.

And that leads us to Step Two.

"If I were
to leave a legacy,
it would be
to live, to learn,
to love and
to laugh."

— STEVEN COVEY,
author

Step Two

Don't be Afraid
to Laugh at
Yourself

"You grow up
the day you
have the
first good laugh
on yourself."

— ETHEL BARRYMORE,
actress

Blessed are they who
can laugh at themselves.
For they shall never
cease to be amused.

You Can Improve Self-Image
by Taking Yourself Lightly

BEING ABLE TO LAUGH AT YOURSELF HAS many ramifications. All of them good. The psychological and emotional benefits are endless.

When you poke fun at yourself it shows you are unafraid to be vulnerable. You become more human in the eyes of others. Laughing at yourself illustrates your exuberant and youthful spirit and people are inclined to like you more. It puts them at ease. Shows humility, one of the most pleasing personality traits a person can possess.

I've seen this simple, practical strategy help many people discover a happier more meaningful life.

Unfortunately, the ability to laugh at ourselves doesn't come naturally. It's an acquired skill. But it's a priceless gift we can easily give ourselves.

The past twenty years have been a golden era in the examination of the effects of humor on the psyche.

Research on the psychological advantages of having a sense of humor has revealed that the willingness to laugh at oneself has many advantages. Self-directed humor:

- Eases tension, anxiety and anger.

- Promotes a feeling of warmth
   and bonding with others.

- Is a coping mechanism associated with
   tolerance, sincerity, wisdom and maturity.

- Is an indication of positive self-esteem
   and emotional health.

- Is a sign of faith in oneself, in people and in
   the world in general.

- And is a counter balance to negative ideas,
   distrust and discouragement.

Many psychologists feel that laughter is a spontaneous burst of affection. Therefore, being able to laugh at oneself is simply a form of expressing self esteem.

Making oneself the butt of a joke in no way diminishes stature or respectability. In fact, the opposite appears to be true. It's really a mature and sensitive form of social behavior.

That self-deprecating humor is a powerful force for winning friends and influencing people is illustrated by the careers of many great comedians.

Woody Allen, Jack Benny, and George Burns are among those who learned early in their careers that when they made themselves the butt of the joke, audiences laughed uproariously. It made the audience feel a kinship. It made the comedians multi-millionaires.

At a testimonial dinner, Jack Benny was presented with an award. He stood before the crowd and said, "I don't deserve this, but I have arthritis and I don't deserve that either."

Carol Burnett, during an Actor's Studio television interview, revealed, "I started my career by being self-deprecating. I would always kid myself before anybody could kid me."

This is not a recent discovery. In ancient times belly laughs were evoked by buffoons, commonly referred to as "fools." The term "fool" was used to describe a person whose absurd and sometimes imbecilic behavior provided continuous entertainment for royalty and nobility.

But those professional fools or court jesters were far from being imbeciles. They were often highly intelligent individuals who dressed up in outlandish costumes and caused shrieks of laughter by blurting out remarks that made them appear dumb or foolish. Most earned their living by making fun of themselves as well as by clever commentary and by ridiculing the pompous and the arrogant. Many gained an enduring reputation for cleverness and wit and won the affection of their masters.

That wit is a sign of perceived intelligence was noted by the English author Arthur Koestler who said, "the jester is brother to the sage."

"All of us
have schnozzles...
if not on our faces,
then in our character,
minds or habits.
When we admit
our schnozzles,
instead of
defending them,
we begin to laugh,
and the world
laughs with us."

—JIMMY DURANTE,
comedian

SELF-DEPRECATING POLITICIANS

We have a rich record of political satire in America. To mock and deride public officials is not merely our delight, it's our duty. Down through the years cartoonists, comedians and humorists have enjoyed a banquet of success criticizing civil servants in a humorous, if pointed, fashion.

Perhaps in an effort to fend off the slings and arrows, some of the most successful politicians have used self-deprecating humor to their advantage.

Recognizing the positive rewards of having voters cackle at their perceived inadequacies, the cleverest politicos have realized that pompous, long-winded speeches don't go over as well as lighter, more humorous fare. Savvy politicians know that substantive ideas go down better if spiced with levity, and most importantly, that good politics and good humor are often inextricably intertwined.

Franklin D. Roosevelt, John F. Kennedy, Ronald Reagan, Mario Cuomo, Colin Powell, Ann Richards, Al Gore and Bill Clinton have all practiced the art of provoking laughter by making themselves the butt of the joke.

Self-disparaging wit is best, for it creates empathy and humanizes one's message. Self-mockery has the added benefit of inoculating one against egomania. And as I've said before, humility is undeniably attractive.

When General Colin Powell speaks, it is said he has the kind of rapport with people that is characteristic of a good politician. Audiences identify with him when he jokes about how he can't even get his wife Alma to make him lunch:

"One of the saddest figures in all Christendom is the Chairman of the Joint Chiefs of Staff, once removed, driving around with a baseball cap pulled over his eyes, making his strategic choice as to whether it's going to be McDonald's or Taco Bell."

"He is not laughed at who laughs at himself first."

— ENGLISH PROVERB

Wherever Mario Cuomo takes the platform, the former Empire State governor is a most welcome speaker. Always good for a big laugh, especially on himself.

These are Cuomo's opening remarks from a speech to the New York Press Club:

"As I left...to come down here tonight, my wife gave me some last-minute advice. She said, 'I know they are a tough group. But don't be intimidated. And don't try to be charming, witty or intellectual. Just be yourself.'"

Ronald Reagan's lifetime in show business helped him in the White House. As an actor he had had many years of perfecting the timing and delivery of scripted lines. Being president was the ultimate opportunity to illustrate his exceptional gift for making people laugh and utilizing his sense of humor to create rapport.

The following exchange, which took place during a news conference in Washington, D.C., personifies Reagan's wit and innate understanding of putting himself down in order to get a laugh:

> *"Mr. President," asked a reporter,*
> *"in talking about the continuing*
> *recession tonight, you have blamed*
> *mistakes of the past, and you've blamed*
> *Congress. Does any of the blame belong*
> *to you?"*
> *"Yes," replied Reagan, "because for*
> *many years I was a Democrat."*

Perhaps Reagan will be best remembered, for making himself the brunt of a joke by his classic remark after having been shot by an attempted assassin:

> *The Chief Executive was in the*
> *operating room surrounded by several*
> *doctors who were preparing to remove*
> *the bullet lodged in his chest. Just as he*
> *was falling asleep from the anesthetic*
> *Reagan looked up at the surgeons and*
> *said, "I hope you guys are all*
> *Republicans."*

"To make mistakes
is human;
to stumble
is commonplace;
to be able to
laugh at yourself
is maturity."

— WILLIAM ARTHUR WARD,
English writer

John F. Kennedy was a master at the self-deprecating joke. When JFK was campaigning for president he was constantly being accused of using his wealthy father's big bucks to get him votes. One day he stood up before a huge crowd in Cleveland and said:

> *"I just received the following telegram from my generous father. It says `Dear Jack, don't buy one single vote more than is necessary.'*
> *"'I'll be damned if I'm going to pay for a landslide!'"*

As a young senator, Kennedy's charisma was recognized by colleagues and foes alike. His special ability to make powerful speeches that inspired audiences all over America gained him great respect from the most demanding critics.

JFK knew one of the major secrets in developing a rapport with crowds was the art of poking fun at himself. Upon receiving an honorary degree at Yale he offered:

> *"It might be said that I now have the best of both worlds — a Harvard education and a Yale degree."*

At SHAPE headquarters in Paris:

> *"I do not think it altogether inappropriate to introduce myself to this audience. I am the man who accompanied Jacqueline Kennedy to Paris — and I have enjoyed it."*

After a speech in Boston:

A young reporter came backstage to meet the handsome senator. Hoping to gain the secret of Kennedy's tremendous power over his audiences the man asked, "What is the last thing you do before you go out to speak? Do you recite a favorite passage in Shakespeare, recall an inspiring bit of Shelley's poetry, or do you think of the intellectual giants down through the ages?"

"None of these," he replied, "I just feel to see if my pants are zipped up."

> "There are three things which are real: God, human folly and laughter. The first two are beyond our comprehension. So we must do what we can with the third."
>
> — JOHN F. KENNEDY
> 35th president

Along with his history-making contributions to humankind, Abraham Lincoln may also have the distinction of being the first American president to have recognized the psychological advantages of self-ridicule.

Mr. Lincoln was never considered a good looking man. In fact, critics of the times often pointed out exactly how homely he was. And yet by creating laughter at his own expense, he turned this seeming deficit into an asset:

> *Lincoln was delivering a speech in his home town, Springfield, Illinois, and a heckler in the back of the crowd shouted up that he was two-faced.*
>
> *Old Abe looked out at the large throng and said to them, "My friends, I ask you, if I had two faces, would I be wearing this one?"*

The newspapers baited him unmercifully. Political foes labeled him an ape and a buffoon. But Lincoln always depended on his keen sense of humor to survive. Here's a story he often told on himself:

> *Two Amish ladies met in the market place. "Who do you think will win the war?" asked the first.*
>
> *"The South," replied the other.*
>
> *"Why?"*
>
> *"Cause I hear Jefferson Davis is a praying man."*
>
> *"But Lincoln is a praying man, too."*
>
> *"Yes, but the Lord will think old Abe is jokin'," said her friend.*

Abraham Lincoln, in his infinite wisdom, a hundred years ahead of the medical researchers, recognized the therapeutic value of laughter.

One morning, while attending an important meeting with members of his cabinet he noticed their stern and sour dispositions. The men he had appointed to help run the country were serious, somber and grim, certainly in no frame of mind to discuss the important issues on the agenda.

The Great Emancipator tried to change the depressing mood with a few humorous anecdotes but to no avail. Then Lincoln uttered the words that have immortalized him as one of the most sensitive and wise American leaders.

"Gentlemen, why don't you laugh? With the fearful strain that is upon me night and day, if I did not laugh, I should die. You need this medicine as much as I do."

"What I value more than all things is good humor."

— THOMAS JEFFERSON, 3rd president

"To be able to laugh
at oneself is rather
more valuable
an accomplishment
than the ability
to laugh at others."

—ASHLEY MONTAGU,
anthropologist

Another chief executive who reveled in the guffaws he provoked with self-effacing humor was Franklin Roosevelt. FDR loved making visitors and the White House staff bust out laughing with stories like this:

> *Mrs. Roosevelt had gone to their doctor for her yearly medical check-up. She came home and announced that she was in perfect physical condition.*
> *"Oh really!" exclaimed Roosevelt. "Didn't the doctor say anything about that big, fat ass of yours?"*
> *"No, Franklin," she replied, "your name was never mentioned."*

Consider how satisfying it must be to reach a stage in life where you are secure enough to hear people laughing at your expense and yet feel good about it.

This was a case where you could say FDR was truly — pardon the pun — the butt of the joke.*

Robert Orben, former director of White House speech writers, observes, "Political leaders embrace humor because humor works. Humor has gone from being an admirable part of a leader's character to a mandatory one."

*More pun fun in Humor 101.

> ## "Any man who has had the job I've had and didn't have a sense of humor wouldn't still be here."
>
> — HARRY TRUMAN,
> 33rd president

When Harry Truman succeeded Roosevelt, the country soon discovered that he too was fearless in the use of self-deprecating humor. Here's a story Truman often told on himself:

A Californian visiting Houston remarked to a native that he heard Truman was going to raise taxes. The Texan stood up and knocked the visitor cold with an uppercut to the jaw.

"What'd you do that for?" asked a bystander. "All he said was 'Truman was raising taxes,'"

"Oh," said the Houstonian. "Ah thought he said Truman was raised in Texas!"

"Most good humor
is self-deprecating.
People enjoy hearing
about the mistakes
you've made.
Nobody's perfect and
when you kid yourself
you come off as a
human being."

—JOE GARAGIOLA,
professional baseball player,
sportscaster

MIRTHFUL MEMORIALS

Somehow the people who are best remembered, the most revered, are the individuals who don't take themselves seriously.

When Duffy Dougherty, the great Michigan State football coach, passed away, fans from all over the sports world recognized him for his contribution to sports as a brilliant leader and motivator of men. But it was *The Associated Press* that noted: "Former coaches, friends and family all agree that Dougherty's coaching accomplishments were overshadowed by his sparkling Irish wit and jovial nature."

Some of us have such a light-hearted-attitude about ourselves that we manage to spread fun and laughter even when we're not alive to hear it.

My attorney, Sam Perlmutter, collects funny wills created for the express purpose of evoking laughter. Here are some favorites:

> *All the relatives were gathered in the lawyer's office anxiously awaiting the reading of their recently departed aunt's will. Each family member figeted nervously, eagerly anticipating a huge financial bequeathement.*
>
> *The attorney donned his specs and said, "Your aunt's will was quite short and to the point. It reads as follows: 'I, Mary Alice Bishop Crenshaw, being of sound mind and bod, spent all my money when I was alive.'"*
>
> *This codicil was in a will left by a departed millionaire:*

"...and to my nephew, Harry, who always said I'd never remember him in my will — 'Hello, Harry!'"

There are many uncommon people who don't take themselves seriously. They derive great pleasure from being playful. A cheerful disposition is a character trait friends and family never forget.

Individuals who are able to joke about themselves erect a monument to their memory that lasts long after they've passed from this earthly scene.

The Los Angeles Times printed this tribute expressed by the manager of an accounting firm about a long time employee who had passed away:

"What set Harriet apart were her exuberance and her joy. She kidded herself and made us laugh. She always had a smile, and she lit up every room she was in. She had a love of people. We truly miss her."

> **"Angels fly because they take themselves lightly."**
>
> — A. NONYMOUS

LEARNING TO LAUGH AT OUR SHORTCOMINGS

Learning to laugh at our imperfections takes the sting out of our insecurities.

Whatever our perceived shortcomings — age, baldness, weight — learning to laugh about them diminishes their negative effect. One sure method of achieving this goal is a self-mocking quip. Here are some that I've collected:

— The overweight woman who said, *"I'm not fat, I'm just three feet too short."*

— A short fella who said, *"I may be a little guy but I save a lot of money. I walk under turnstiles."*

— The senior who said, *"As I get older I'm finding that either my eyes are getting bad or my arms are too short."*

— The bald guy who said, *"Haven't I got a beautiful head of skin?"* And,

— *"God made a lot of heads, and those he was ashamed of he covered up with hair."*

It isn't necessary to constantly put yourself down but self-deprecating humor shows that you're human. It also reveals that you're self-assured.

It keeps you from taking yourself too seriously and makes dealing with others easier.

Harvey Mackay, in his book *Dig Your Well Before You're Thirsty* describes a meeting with boxing great Mohammad Ali. The champ had been suffering from Parkinson's, a debilitating disease. Yet he still managed to exhibit a sense of humor and poke fun at himself.

"I was ushered into the champs office," writes McKay. "Mohammed rose from behind the desk to shake my hand. 'Hi,' he whispered, 'I'm Joe Frazier.'"

"Man is distinguished
from all other
creatures
by the facility
of laughter."

—JOSEPH ADDISON,
English essayist, poet

"When things aren't
going very well,
you've got to be able
to laugh at yourself.
Having a
sense of humor
is tantamount
to success."

—AL ROSEN,
professional baseball player
and team executive

How's Your Laugh Life?

SOME PEOPLE PRIDE THEMSELVES on their sense of humor whether they have one or not. Others don't give themselves the credit they deserve.

Here's a chance to test yourself. Answer YES or NO to each of the questions:

	YES	NO
1. Do you feel that a great many of the jokes people tell you are somewhat pointless?	____	____
2. A well-known psychiatrist says, "In overcoming our fears, a sense of humor is even more important than will power." Do you think this statement should be taken with a grain of salt?	____	____
3. Do you think the world would not be in the shape it is today if people took things a little more seriously?	____	____

4. In looking at cartoons in a
   newspaper or magazine, do
   you look for errors the
   cartoonist may have made?   ____   ____

5. Does it make you angry when
   someone makes you lose your
   dignity?   ____   ____

6. Do you hate to tell a joke on
   yourself?   ____   ____

7. Do you think the importance
   of having a sense of humor is
   frequently overrated?   ____   ____

8. When someone else is telling
   a funny story are you often
   so busy trying to think of
   one yourself that you only
   half listen?   ____   ____

9. Do you think that people
   who do things just for the
   fun of it are likely to be
   irresponsible?   ____   ____

10. A famous poet once said,
    "Wrinkle not thy face
    with too much laughter
    lest thou become
    ridiculous." Does this
    strike you as sound advice?   ____   ____

SCORING:

For each question answered with a YES, you get a score of nothing. Every question answered with a NO, give yourself 10 points.

RATE YOURSELF:

Less than 50 points — You are an extremely serious person, inclined to view things too literally. And though you have some sense of humor, you haven't given it a chance to develop.

50 — 60 points — You have a fair sense of humor.

70 points — Average. Psychologists point out that the average person's sense of humor is not all that it might be. They agree that you would be happier if you would take things less seriously.

80 points — Good.

90-100 points — Excellent. Things don't bother you much if you score this high for you have learned to laugh at yourself. Congratulations!

NOTHING SUCCEEDS LIKE LAUGHTER

Stephen R. Covey, author of *The 7 Habits of Highly Effective People,* provides practical tips on achieving lofty career goals. He suggests developing strong relationships with family and friends, listening to co-workers, customers, and suppliers, and adhering to a program of continuing education in your field. He writes, "Focus your efforts on those areas that you can truly influence and **smile** about those that, for now, are outside your influence."

Psychologists have discovered that successful companies and successful families share many of the same attributes. They are open, democratic, relaxed and playful. And they are humorous.

Most high achievers have that uncanny ability to recognize things they cannot change and are able to smile about it. They also seem to have the propensity to make jokes that expose their vulnerabilities.

Former major league baseball catcher Joe Garagiola jokes about his lifetime batting average of only .257. "Each year I don't play I get better! The first year on the banquet trail I was a former ballplayer. The second year I was great. The third year one of baseball's stars. And last year I was introduced as one of baseball's immortals. The older I get the more I realize that the worst break I had was playing."

I asked Joe if the players had a sense of humor. "Most of the guys I played ball with took what they did and what they said very seriously, but didn't take themselves seriously. "

> ## "Laugh at yourself first, before anybody else can."
>
> — ELSA MAXWELL,
> columnist

Lee Iacocca, former president of Chrysler and one of the most famous businessmen of the 20th century, tells about the time he was at an expensive restaurant in San Francisco. He was in the men's room when a fellow approached him:

> *"Mr. Iacocca, I'm your greatest admirer. I've read your books. I've studied your career. What success I've had comes from emulating you."*
> *Iacocca thanked him.*
> *"Could I ask a favor of you, please?" said the man. "I'm sitting with some colleagues. Would you walk by my table*

*and say, 'Hello, Jack' and let me introduce
you. It would mean so much to me."*

Iacocca agreed.

*A few minutes later he walked
toward the table with a smile on his face.
One of Jack's friend's said, "Good
heavens, it's Lee Iacocca and he's heading
this way."*

*Just then Iacocca arrived at the table
and said, "Hello, Jack. Introduce me to
your friends."*

*"Lee, could you come back later,"
snapped Jack. "We're having lunch right
now!"*

Self-deprecating humor is liberating. It frees us
from pomposity, arrogance and self-importance.

Self-directed humor allows us to achieve the
ultimate in life — the satisfaction that comes with
self-respect and a positive self-image. When we
feel good about ourselves, when we're confident,
everything else usually falls into place.

"If I were given the
opportunity to
present a gift
to the next generation,
it would be the
ability for each
individual to learn
to laugh at himself."

— CHARLES SCHULTZ,
cartoonist

Step Three

Bite Adversity
in the Butt
(Before it Bites You)

"Having a light-hearted
attitude enables
you to keep your
perspective.
It's amazing how
you can relieve
the tension when
you help people
lighten up."

—THOMAS A. MERCER,
Rear Admiral USN (RET.)

Humor is the hole that
lets the hot air out
of a stuffed shirt.

You Can Conquer
the Alligators With a
Light-Hearted Attitude

THE ONLY THING CERTAIN IN TODAY'S rock'em sock'em world of commerce is uncertainty. What worked yesterday is a formula for failure tomorrow. Tried and true tenets of business that helped past generations to the top — the cookie-cutter gray suit, anything-for-the-corporation mind set—is doomed in the 21st century.

The world has undergone dramatic transformations. Markets have amorphosized into fluid global networks. Job security as we once knew it has gone the way of the village blacksmith. *Teamwork* and *change* are operative words now.

In this new cooperative era, individual heroics are not nearly as important as how well a person performs as a creative member of a dynamic team.

Change is occurring with mind-boggling speed. Nothing in business seems anchored on solid ground — almost everything is cast adrift. But one element of this stress-producing equation remains constant and can serve as the rudder to steady our boats through the raging seas.

No matter what challenges we face, no matter what obstacles or adversity we encounter or how many alligators we meet, a light-hearted attitude is our most potent, dependable tool for surviving and thriving.

A sharp sense of humor gives the mind flexibility to cope with the unexpected. It is perhaps the singularly most important requirement for achieving success and happiness.

A light-hearted attitude counters the heavy-handed approach to business and helps to cultivate a positive work environment that enables us to maximize creativity and productivity.

> "Laughter need not be cut out of anything, since it improves everything."
>
> —JAMES THURBER,
> author

THE POWER OF PERSPECTIVE ON THE JOB

Humor is like a beacon. When we are light-hearted, people are attracted by the light. Our cheerfulness has a great affect on others.

Studies show that people doing tasks with a joyful sprit and a buoyant attitude do a better job.

Humor in the workplace gets positive results.

A spirited outlook takes no special talent or ability, no physical prowess or skill, no Ph.D or license. What's more, it feels good, it's fun, it's fat free and it doesn't require batteries.

Humor and its ability to neutralize job stress has been the subject of much investigation. There is scientific evidence that suggests laughter may actually transform a tense workplace into a relaxed environment that improves productivity. Humor appears to be a magic bullet against stress.

A Southern Illinois University study reveals that "humor has the potential to help one put stressful situations into a less threatening perspective."

Researchers on the Laughter Project at the University of California Santa Barbara found that "laughter did as well in reducing stress as more complex biofeedback training programs did."

Imagine. Smiles, chuckles, and good solid belly laughs offer the miraculous physical phenomenon of making us feel good all over, putting a twinkle in our eyes, and calming the raging storms that threaten our job performance.

That humor can so dramatically alter the atmosphere at work is not so surprising. We all know how awful it feels to be subjected to a co-worker's ill-temper; or to be stressed out over deadlines or other job-related pressures.

These are anxiety-producing circumstances in the workplace that beg comic relief. Just as in the movies, a well-timed laugh is the best and fastest counter balance for on-the-job tension.

"Humor can be
used as a far more
effective way of altering
employee behavior
than delivering
a list of do's and don'ts
which can put people
on the defensive."

—JOHN CLEESE
actor, screenwriter

HOW DO YOU SEE THE WORLD?

Is your intuitive recognition negative or positive? Is the glass half empty or half full?

> *An elderly man owned a gas station in a small town. At age 77, he had become somewhat philosophical about life. An easy-going-kind-of-guy, even strangers liked to talk to him.*
>
> *One day a family moving into town stopped for gas and asked him if the town was friendly. "How was it where you lived before?" asked the old man.*
>
> *"Just awful. The people were rude, unfriendly, mean-spirited, terrible human beings."*
>
> *"Yeah," said the septuagenarian. "I think you'll find that it's like that here, too."*
>
> *They soon discovered he was right.*
>
> *Later, another family moved into the area and stopped for gas. "Is this town, friendly?"*
>
> *"How was it where you used to live?"*
>
> *"Oh, a lovely town. Good neighbors, generous, kind, caring and community spirited."*
>
> *"Well," said the senior, "you'll find it's like that here, too."*
>
> *And they, too, discovered that the old man was right.*

Good or bad, the world usually reflects back to us what we project. If we treat people with respect and cheerfulness, most will treat us the same way. It's human nature.

When people smile at us — we smile back. When they are courteous and sociable we usually respond in kind. When we bring a smile to work it creates far reaching positive consequences.

How much of our success depends on our attitude?

Futurist Watts Wacker sees it this way: "An optimist usually has a good future; a pessimist usually has a bad future. Yet, the very same things usually happen to both of them."

Have you ever noticed that when you wake up feeling cheerful, with a positive attitude toward yourself and high expectations of the coming day, somehow the world takes on a much different tone?

The people you come in contact with are of good cheer and in a happy frame of mind, or they become that way when you're with them.

You see, it is possible to spread this light-hearted attitude. To carry it over into your work, pass it on to the people you meet every day. What a powerful force for success it is!

> "Life is like a sewer. What you get out of it depends on what you put into it."
>
> —TOM LEHERER,
> humorist

"A light-hearted attitude
helps you over the
rough spots.
Life isn't a smooth
four-lane highway.
It's got a lot of pot holes.
When you hit a pot hole,
you get a flat tire,
there's no sense
moanin' and groanin'.
Find something funny
about it and it'll
help you get over it."

— JOE GARAGIOLA,
professional baseball player
sportscaster

FINDING FUN IN FOUL-UPS

The movers and shakers of the world don't always concur. But most do agree on one aspect of business: the bottom line depends on good customer service.

A sign prominently displayed on the desk of an Arizona auto dealer says:

> *Customer service means*
> *you're still polite to the customer*
> *even after the check clears.*

Foul-ups happen all the time. But when the problem is acknowledged, corrected, and handled with good humor, the customer's resentment is neutralized. Case in point:

> *At the Newark airport, a United Airlines flight was canceled and all the passengers were lined up at the gate to book another flight. Suddenly, a man pushed his way up to the front of the line, slapped his ticket on the desk and yelled at the woman behind the counter, "I have to be on this next flight and it has to be in first class."*
>
> *"I'll be happy to help you," she said, "but all these people in line are ahead of you."*
>
> *He sneered and shouted, "Do you have any idea who I am?"*
>
> *The agent grabbed her public address microphone and said, "Attention, please! We have a passenger here who does not know who he is. If anyone can help him find his identity, please come to the gate."*

Everybody standing in line began to laugh. The guy was furious and cursed at the agent using the F-word. He yelled, "F____ you!"

Without flinching, she just smiled and said, "I'm sorry, sir, but you'll have to stand in line for that, too."

As this irate Mr. Smooth stormed away the other passengers began applauding. Although the flight was canceled and passengers were inconvenienced, one witty United employee had lightened a tense situation and redeemed the company with the use of humor.

Successful people recognize that a light approach is a way a life. They strive to manage body, mind, heart and spirit as effectively as they manage business.

> **"Laughter is the shortest distance between two people."**
>
> — VICTOR BORGE, comedian

"It's much better
to have fun
in life than
not have fun.
I don't believe that
you have to be
boring to be
successful."

— Herb Kelleher, chairman
Southwest Airlines

LIGHTER IS BETTER

The executive recruiting firm of Robert Half International conducted a survey among personnel directors and vice presidents in 1000 of the largest corporations. Here's what they learned:

"Eighty four out of one hundred respondents agreed that people with a sense of humor do better at their jobs than those with little or no sense of humor.

"They tend to be more creative, less rigid and more willing to consider and embrace new ideas and methods."

Adopting a lighter attitude on the job is conducive to a high level of professionalism, competence and responsibility.

Margery Tippen, a *Sprint* executive in Dallas, makes this observation: "We believe employees who have fun feel appreciated and come together as a team. That helps them be more productive and helps our customers."

A Philadelphia insurance company exec raves about a retired colleague's behavior in the workplace: "I always knew when Patti was in the office, because you could hear her laugh a mile away. She had a way of smoothing difficult situations with laughs, smiles and good nature."

FIVE REASONS TO PUT MORE HUMOR IN THE WORKPLACE

There are many benefits to encouraging a light-hearted attitude at work. Humor helps the workplace function smoothly.

1. It's not only fun, it's infectious. Shared humor draws employees together and creates a bond.

2. It not only influences the quality of our work, it affects how others feel about us.

3. It's the simplest, easiest, most efficient way for people to work more effectively as a team.

4. A light-hearted attitude produces an atmosphere conducive to problem solving.

5. It's an effective way of neutralizing conflicts.

6. We are more productive and better team players when we're loose and feel free from stress.

7. A light-hearted attitude keeps us flexible and helps us face frustrations and pressures.

"If you create an
atmosphere
for fun you'll get
good work."

—JOSEPH MANKIEWICZ,
screenwriter, producer, director,
(told to Jerry Lewis before
directing his first motion picture).
—*The Total Film Maker*

A friend of mine was a victim of corporate cutbacks at a Silicon Valley computer firm — one of the least funny facts of life in business today. Yet he recounts his experience with humor. He found out he was unemployed when the CEO stopped him in the hallway:

> *"I've decided to use humor in*
> *in the workplace," said the boss.*
> *"Experts claim humor eases tension,*
> *which is very important when there is*
> *downsizing and the work force is being*
> *trimmed. Knock-knock!"*
> *"Who's there?" said my friend.*
> *"Not you anymore."*

> ## "Laughter is like a passionate kiss ... it excites us and makes us feel good."
>
> — PAUL J. ROSCH, MD,
> Clinical Professor of Medicine and
> Psychiatry, New York Medical College

Mark McCormick, the eminent sports manager, in his best-seller, *What They Don't Teach You at Harvard Business School,* makes specific reference to the importance of levity in business.

"Laughter is the most potent constructive force for defusing business tension. It's the best way to start off a meeting. You don't have to have them falling in the aisles, but a mildly pleasant remark at the outset will create the right atmosphere for everything that follows."

Bill Walsh, the former coach of the San Francisco 49ers, is famed for having won three Super Bowl titles. In his book, *Building a Champion,* Walsh describes one remedy for the paralyzing tension before a kickoff.

"As a coach you're almost operating on nerve the 48 hours before the game. You're trying to keep things light. With the 49ers there was a lot of humor in our meetings. An inexperienced player will have a problem with anxiety, so anything that relieves that pressure is beneficial."

Perhaps no profession is fraught with greater on-the-job stress than professional sports. In pro football, anxiety is an integral part of the game. Players are under pressure to produce or be terminated. Added to the worry about job security is the constant threat of injury, sometimes life threatening, often career ending.

Then there are the infinitely complex relationships between athletes and coaches where anger, hostility, and racial differences all come into play. The head coach must overcome all these obstacles to keep players focused and motivated.

Vince Lombardi, the immortal coach of the Green Bay Packers, knew how to handle his players. Often he relied on humor. In response to racial tension that threatened to divide the team

Lombardi called his squad together in the dressing room. "Listen, you guys!" he said. "There are only three colors here. Green, Gold and Italian."

"A jest often
decides matters
of importance
more effectively
and happily
than seriousness."

—HORACE.
Roman lyric poet and satirist

EASING THE STRESS SYNDROME

A *Wall Street Journal* article quoted a report by the United Nations International Labor Organization:

"Stress has become one of the most serious health issues of the 20th Century.

"Job stress is a world-wide plague that afflicts British miners and Swedish waitresses just as it burns out Japanese teachers and American executives.

"Stress sets up a vicious cycle. A worker leaves a stressful home life, builds up more stress during a commute to the job, works eight hours in a stressful environment, has another stressful commute home, then unloads on his family who — naturally — react with anger."

Stress is responsible for two-thirds of all office visits to doctors. There is evidence that work-related tension and "raw nerves" may contribute to everything from heart disease and cancer to the common cold.

A key to overcoming emotional depression is to deal with it positively. First we must understand that stress happens when we allow changes, pressures and demands to adversely affect us. This triggers a fear response.

The same basic physical reactions occur when we laugh as do when we are overcome with fear. In both instances the blood pumps faster, the heart rate climbs and the adrenal glands go crazy. In both mirth and fright we are stressed. That is, disrupted mentally or emotionally.

The major difference is that laughter provides pleasure. Something we can eagerly anticipate enjoy and remember. It gives us reward and satisfaction. This pleasant panacea of humor increases our willingness to take risks and try new things.

We live in a harried, hurried, pressure-packed world. Anxiety is part of everybody's life. But it can be managed by changing the way we think, by developing a more relaxed, joyful point of view.

The philosopher William James makes it all seem so simple when he writes: "Human beings can alter their lives by altering their attitudes of mind."

> "Organize a hum-a-long at work. It's hard to feel stressed when you're humming."
>
> — DONNA STRICKLAND,
> health care consultant

There are many clinical definitions of stress. My favorite is hung on the wall of my doctor's office:

STRESS
The condition that arises when
your brain overrides your body's
desire to choke the living crap out of
some turkey who desperately deserves it.

We can deal with stress in a variety of ways, from jogging and paddle ball to biofeedback, aerobics and herbal tea. All these methods work to some extent. But the quickest, most effective way to beat stress is simply to get some good laughs.

At a *Humor in the Workplace* seminar I conducted for AT&T in Palm Beach, a young V.P. asked, "If I have a tense situation coming up — an important meeting, a presentation, anything stressful — how can I deal with that immediately?"

My recommendation is the same for busy executives as it is for stay-at-home parents or retirees:

FIVE STRATEGIES TO BREAK THE STRESS CYCLE

1. Schedule a 10 minute humor break.

2. Sit back, relax, put your feet up.

3. Take a three deep breaths.

4. Read something funny — a humorous article, some cartoons, jokes, perhaps listen to a comedian on a cassette.

5. Make it a point to laugh out loud.

Amazing how a couple of good laughs will loosen up the knot in your shoulders, boost your spirits and create a winning attitude.

The bottom line is to meet a challenge head on by establishing a tension-free atmosphere.

"A sense of humor
is part of the art
of leadership,
of getting along
with people,
of getting
things done."

— DWIGHT D. EISENHOWER,
34th president

*DON'T LOSE YOUR
SENSE OF HUMOR
by Jimmy Durante

When stormy clouds surround you
And troubles all around you
And when you feel your fate is sealed and signed
Don't lose your sense of humor
And you won't lose your peace of mind.

When lady luck has brushed you
And Fortune's really crushed you
And when you feel that everything's been tried
Don't lose your sense of humor
And you'll see the sunny side.

   I have heard for sure
   For troubles they have a cure
   Take a teaspoon full of smiles
   And add some laughter
   There's nothing like a laugh
   To cut your troubles right in half
   And live happily ever after.

So when you see the lightning
It really isn't frightening
A flash, a fraction then the flash is out.
Don't lose your sense of humor
And you'll find without a doubt
Soon you'll have something to shout about.

*With permission by The Jimmy Durante
Music Publishing Company.

105

HUMOR IS A COPING STRATEGY

It's the end of a long stressful day. You've had one crisis after another at the office, a bumper-to-bumper traffic nightmare commute. How do you relieve the pressure at the end of such a day?

Wouldn't it be nice to unwind BEFORE you got home so that you could walk through the door refreshed and smiling?

You can.

While you're driving plug in a comedy cassette or CD. Get some good belly laughs under your belt. You'll decompress by the time you arrive home, be relaxed, and in a better frame of mind, ready to enjoy your family.

> "A good laugh
> is sunshine in
> a house."
>
> — WILLIAM MAKEPEACE THACKERY
> (1811-1863)

BETTER LAUGHERS MAKE BETTER BOSSES

Immediately following my presentation to management at Hewlett-Packard one of the execs came up to the podium. "The best boss I ever had is now one of the most successful businessmen in this country," he offered. "Yet with all his wealth and success, his most admirable trait was his great sense of humor.

"This guy had a knack for keeping the workplace light. As a boss he could be demanding, but you didn't mind knocking yourself out for him because he was the kind of guy who made you feel good. A guy you liked whether he was your boss or not."

Over and over, successful executives have told me how the magic of mirth in the workplace is a unifying common denominator. The boss who displays a sense of humor is embraced as a member of the team, a person who is genuinely liked.

And that spirit, that light-hearted enthusiasm, fires up the creative juices, boosts productivity and improves communication. It also inspires loyalty and respect.

What a great way to get the job done!

The question is *how* do you develop a light-hearted attitude?

That leads us to Step Four.

"Have fun...
Anything can change
without warning,
and that's why
I try not to take any
of what's happened
too seriously.

— DONALD TRUMP,
entrepreneur

Step Four

Expose Yourself
to Humor Every Day

"Laughter is our
only salvation.
Pray with a giggle
and mourn with a smile.
And if you happen
to believe, as I do,
that women are
nature's noblest work,
know ye that
long face never won
fair lady."

— LAWRENCE SANDERS,
author

A good laugh is like
manure to a farmer
— it doesn't do any good
until you spread it around.

You Can Laugh Yourself
to Mental Agility
and Longer Life

GETTING INTO THE HABIT OF LAUGHING OUT loud, learning to laugh at yourself and nurturing a light-hearted attitude are necessary steps to take when you're up to your eyeballs in alligators. Becoming aware of the humor around you is equally important.

Expose yourself to something funny every day. It's just as vital to exercise your funny bone as it is to give your body a regular workout.

People who understand and appreciate the value of humor often carry a favorite cartoon around in their wallets, pin something funny on the office wall. Anything to make laughter an integral part of their daily lives.

Laughter helps us see the universe as a friendlier habitat. It makes the world a place of infinite possibility rather than a dead-end street.

A chuckle or grin breaks mental and emotional gridlock. Laughing lubricates our creative joints, lightens our worldly load, and puts a pleasant spin on the way we view our lives.

The human brain is the most awesome computer ever created. When we put in funny thoughts today it stores them up for a rainy day. Then when we need humor most it is there for us like second nature.

Professionals who earn their livings making people laugh steep themselves in comedy. They know that the more humor they absorb, the easier it is to think funny on their feet.

In the interview with Johnny Carson for my book, *The Great Comedians Talk About Comedy,* we discussed the ability to ad-lib. "The more jokes and lines you know," said Carson, "the better equipped you are to say something funny when you need it."

I asked, "When a specific situation presents itself to ad-lib, do you consciously think of the funny comment before you deliver it or does it just come out?"

He replied with this example: "We had a fellow on the show, a writer, weighed five hundred pounds, big guy. One of the guests on the show, a girl said, 'I wanted to be a nun.' And this writer who was sitting there said, 'I always wanted to be a monk.' And I said, almost without thinking, 'You could be a monastery.'

"Now that may not be the funniest joke in the world but at the time it fitted perfectly. I didn't stop and think. It just came out. The audience roared."

"The creator made man
able to do everything —
talk, run, look and hear.
He was not satisfied,
though, until man
could do just one
thing more —and
that was LAUGH.
And so man
laughed and laughed.
And the creator said,
'Now you are fit to live.'"

— APACHE MYTH

RELATIONSHIPS REQUIRE COMIC RELIEF

Humor is the icing on the cake in having a successful relationship. Many people rank a good sense of humor at or near the top of qualities they most desire in a friend, business associate or significant other.

Newspaper personals are rife with examples of people seeking humorous partners:

> **Classy F**, 28, artist, seeks WM
> with zany sense of humor who
> likes art, sports and loves to laugh.

> **Businessman**, 50ish, Handsome,
> Vegetarian, WM, 44, tender, funny,
> linguist. Seeks slim, loyal
> WF 35 who loves dancing,
> dining and laughter.

Leigh Weimers, the popular San Jose Mercury News columnist, writes lovingly about the marriage of his daughter who had met her husband while they were both Peace Corps volunteers in Togo, West Africa:

"They knew they were in love, their friend told me at the ceremony, because 'Karin never laughed as heartily or as long as she did when she was with Bill.'

"It takes a sense of humor to get through life, in stressful foreign climes or in the benign surroundings of home, and that gift they share is the greatest that any young couple could enjoy."

British author W. Somerset Maughm wrote adoringly of his mother. In biographical notes he related various remembrances as a boy growing up in France, emphasizing the strong relationship shared by his mother and father.

"My mother was much admired. She was a very beautiful woman and my father was a very ugly man. They were known in the Paris of that day as Beauty and the Beast.

"Mother's close friend, Lady Anglesley, once said to her, 'You're so beautiful and there are so many people in love with you, why are you faithful to that ugly little man you're married to?'

"And my mother answered, 'He never hurts my feelings — and he makes me laugh.'"

> ## "Laughter is the handshake of communication."
>
> — LOLA GILLEBAARD,
> humorist

"Pointing out the
comic elements
of a situation
can bring a sense of
proportion and
perspective
to what
might otherwise
seem an
overwhelming
problem."

— HARVEY MINDESS,
psychologist

PARENTS PASSING LAUGHTER TO PRODIGIES

Humor is the glue that keeps families together, cements friendships, and strengthens marriages. Appreciating humor together adds a special dimension to life.

One priceless legacy parents can pass on to their offspring is a sense of humor. Making children aware of what's funny and encouraging them to laugh is a gift that will last forever.

It's just as important for parents to laugh with their kids every day as it is to read them stories, make sure they eat their vegetables and do their homework.

Learning to appreciate what your children think is funny allows you to connect with them better. Prize-winning author Annie Dillard, in *An American Childhood,* a lively memoir of her growing up in Pittsburgh during the 1950's, writes:

"Our parents would sooner have left us out of Christmas than leave us out of a joke. They explained a joke to us while they were still laughing at it; they tore a still-kicking joke apart, so we could see how it worked."

Comedian Rosie O'Donnell talked about her childhood in a Parade Magazine interview:

"In our family, any show of emotion was frowned upon, other than humor. You could communicate what you were feeling as long as you could make a joke about it."

"Once I wore a T-shirt to school in December, because nobody told me to wear a sweater. The teacher embarrassed me in front of all the kids. I made it into a funny story at the dinner table. You could change reality of a painful situation through comedy, but you couldn't cry. That wasn't an option."

Robert Ward, a California writer, pays tribute to his mom in these Mother's Day reflections:

"My mom was there at the beginning of my life, with a laugh, teaching me how to develop one of life's greatest treasures — a gutsy sense of humor.

"She says that 'having fun is good for the soul. If you stop laughing they'll start shoveling dirt on you.'

"When my mother is ready for the dirt, I'll be there for her, with a laugh, a token offering of my thanks to her for showing me that life is indeed better, richer and easier with a sense of humor in hand."

> "Without laughter,
> life on our
> planet would
> be intolerable."
>
> — STEVE ALLEN,
> comedian

BECOME MORE AWARE OF HUMOR

Start doing things differently. Vary daily routines. See the absurdity in your day. View experiences from a humorous standpoint.

Try doing something counter intuitive.

How we've always looked at things doesn't have to be the only way. By changing long-ingrained habits we develop new perceptions.

The very act of altering customary patterns paves the way for fresh ideas. Breaking old practices is a process to begin seeing things from a more amusing angle.

Consider what happens when you discover a new word. You hear it for the first time. It's not familiar. You look it up in the dictionary. Then suddenly you begin to see and hear that word everywhere. Your awareness has been enlarged.

In the same way, when we can expose ourselves to something funny every day and become aware of the comic absurdity around us, our world expands.

> "Life literally abounds in comedy, if you just look around you."
>
> — MEL BROOKS,
> writer, actor, film maker

PEOPLE ARE FUNNY

Listen to others and notice their behavior. Observing and tuning in to fellow humans is a simple way to sharpen our wits.

Eavesdropping in public places is a source of endless entertainment. Human beings often spill their souls in the most public places without realizing their words and actions may be observed.

Wherever we travel, my wife and I enjoy being the proverbial flies on the wall. It's fascinating what one can learn. It costs nothing. We are privy to intimate secrets the perpetrators will never know we know.

We've noticed the most amusing, amazing sights in hotel lobbies around the world and overheard enough scintillating conversation to keep us in comic fodder for ten lifetimes. As writers and inveterate students of human behavior, people-watching is our favorite pastime and an infinite source of material.

While heading to a gate at New York's John F. Kennedy airport, a couple carrying heavy luggage were scurrying alongside me. This is what I overheard:

> *"I'm so excited," puffed the woman,*
> *"We're finally going to Florida on*
> *vacation."*
> *"Yeah," said the man. "I just*
> *wish the piano was here."*
> *"What do you want the piano for?"*
> *"That's where I left the plane tickets."*

People *are* funny. They provide endless entertainment for the tuned-in observer.

Here are some pearls from my collection:

A passenger on a Crystal Harmony cruise sailing through the inland passageway of Alaska:

"My allergy is so much better since we sailed. What is the altitude here?"

In a Chicago Chinese restaurant:

"It's not the egg roll, Morris, it's our whole life."

Conversation between two big-time corporate types sitting in first class on a United flight from Washington, D. C. to Los Angeles:

"What do you think is the main problem with our society today — is it ignorance or apathy?"
"I don't know and I don't care!"

> **"Laughter is the music of life."**
> — SIR WILLIAM OSLER,
> Canadian physician

INCONGRUITIES ARE FERTILE GROUND FOR FUN

People often don't realize what they are saying. Sometimes, what's on our minds is completely different from what trips off our tongues:

"Health is a wonderful thing to have, especially when you're sick."

"Isn't it a pity that the Lovells have no children?"
"It certainly is, but I hear that sterility is hereditary on both sides of their family."

No list of humorous incongruities would be complete without contributions from one of America's great original philosophers, Hall of Fame Yankee catcher, Yogi Berra:

"You can observe a lot just by watching."

"When you get to the fork in the road, take it."

"If you don't know where you are going you could wind up somewhere else."

In presenting an award to New York Yankees great Joe DiMaggio, Berra said:

"Joe, I want to thank you for teaching me that the only way to do something correctly, is to do it right."

PEARLS FOR PRYING EARS

Malapropisms are the ridiculous misuse of words that are similar in sound.

Sometimes people who aren't familiar with the meaning of certain words misapply them. What comes out instead almost always turns out to be quite laughable:

> *The American government finally decided to put all the Indians in reservoirs.*

> *Cleopatra died when an ass bit her.*

> *The trouble with the world today is over-copulation.*

One of the most celebrated malapropists was the legendary Hollywood producer Sam Goldwyn. Here's his best known assault on the English language:

> *"Anybody who'd go to a psychiatrist ought to have his head examined."*

However, the beloved San Francisco columnist Herb Caen believed that Californian Vivian Clore, who lived to be 99, deserved the title of all-time champion. Here are some of Aunt Vivian's contributions:

> *"I like the convenience of my precious cooker."*

*"Did you know that Mt. St. Helens
hasn't had an erection in 123 years?"*

"I just love that Gaucho Marx."

*"Good news, they finally freed
the hostriches in Iran."*

*"One of my daughters was married
in Taco, New Mexico."*

Caen also listed the one-time San Francisco Supervisor James B. Sheehy as a well-known malapropper.

*"This is crouched in language
that is perfectly oblivious."*

*"This defecation of character
must cease."*

And here's the definitive malaprop from the lips of a New Jersey Congressman uttered before 1,622 of his constituents at a gala fund raising dinner in Jersey City:

*"Just remember this, my friends!
As long as I am in the senate, there
will never be a nuclear suppository
in North New Jersey."*

"Instead of working
for the survival
of the fittest,
we should be
working for
the survival
of the wittiest;
then we can
all die laughing."

— LILY TOMLIN,
comedian, actress

FUNNY STORIES ARE EVERYWHERE

Listening to men and women in a cocktail lounge, at a bar or a party, one hears humorous tales. They can be true anecdotes, or they might be jokes. It doesn't make any difference. The important thing is to keep a sharp ear out for the humor around us.

Always on the alert for a good tale, I overheard this gem while waiting for a plane connection in the Atlanta Airport Red Carpet Lounge. Two salesmen were also whiling away the time, and one of them told this story:

A fella decides to take up sky diving. On his first attempt, he jumps out of the plane, drops 3,000 feet, pulls the ripcord, and the chute doesn't open. He falls another 3,000 feet, yanks on the the ripcord, and the chute still doesn't open.

The poor guy is plummeting to the ground, faster and faster. He looks down, and there's a black dot coming up towards him, It turns out to be another guy. And as he goes by, he grabs him and says, "Hey! Do you know anything about parachutes?"

The other guy says, "No! Do you know anything about butane stoves?"

"Laughter
is God's hand
in a
troubled world."

— MINNIE PEARL,
comedian

THE BEST TV COMMERCIALS ARE FUNNY

They are another easy source for a daily dose of laughter.

Television commercials are seen over and over by millions of viewers. In the barrage of marketing mayhem which commercials do we remember? Which ones are the most effective?

The TV commercials that are most talked about at the water cooler are humorous. The ones that make us smile are the ones that leave a lasting impression.

Some of the best commercial catch phrases still evoke a chuckle:

"I can't believe I ate the whole thing!"

"Mother, please, I'd rather do it my self!"

"Where's the beef?"

Video Storyboard Tests, Inc. does an annual survey of 22,000 viewers who are asked to name outstanding advertising. "Humor in advertising still sells well after all these years," says David Vadehra, Video Storyboard's President.

Advertising agencies will practically kill to create TV spots we will watch. These people aren't idiots. They know we turn off commercials unless there's something compelling to hold our attention, a message with entertainment value, of which the most successful are humorous.

These are the ones the public will sit through and actually enjoy. Madison Avenue knows that making such an emotional connection with potential customers is the best way to warm them up to a product.

"Joking decides
great things
stronger and
better oft
than earnest can."

— OLD ENGLISH SAYING

VARIETY IS THE SPICE OF LAUGHTER

It's easy to expose yourself to something funny every day. But not all of us find the same things amusing. Fortunately, today's marketplace offers something for every taste, from whoopee cushions to humorous greeting cards.

Novelty stores sell funny posters and bumper stickers, cartoons, memos, greeting cards, laugh-a-day calendars, T-shirts, mugs, goofy hats, Groucho glasses, clown noses and adult toys.

There's no excuse to be grumpy, even when you have to pay bills. There are checkbooks designed to take the pain out of paying. A checkbook titled, "Smiles" is printed with round smiley faces. And "Coffee Break" with pre-stained checks for your convenience.

> **"Laughter
> can be heard
> farther
> than weeping."**
>
> **—YIDDISH PROVERB**

LEVITY LEADS TO LONGEVITY

When you expose yourself to something funny every day you expand your consciousness to the wider world of humor. In addition, you may also extend your life span.

Laughter "is related in several ways to longevity," according to psychologist Jeffrey Goldstein of Temple University.

It may seem farfetched to suppose that an occasional guffaw can have beneficial cardiovascular effects the way jogging or strenuous exercise can. "But in a real physiological way," states the University of California, Berkeley Wellness Letter, "it may reduce stress, hypertension, and depression, hearts attacks and strokes," thereby slowing up the aging process.

According to Dr. William Fry of Stanford, laughter increases respiratory activity, oxygen exchange, muscular activity and heart rate.

In addition, Dr. Fry points out that, "it stimulates the cardiovascular, respiratory, endocrine and nervous systems, the pituitary and adrenal glands, as well as production of endorphins in the brain."

Another theory is that laughter stimulates the brain to produce hormones called catecholamines, such as epinephrine, norepinephrine and dopamine. These hormones may then trigger the release of endorphins, natural opiates, that can reduce pain or discomfort from arthritis or chronic allergy.

The production of beta-endorphins that cause "runner's high" also brings about the "laugher's high."

Psychological studies show that the older individual with a well-developed sense of humor is more flexible and has healthier mechanisms for coping with life's difficulties.

FOUR IMPORTANT WAYS HUMOR SLOWS AGING

1. It helps to defuse the anger or frustration associated with a distressing event by focusing on its comical elements.

2. Humor enables the elderly to alter the perception of situations which could otherwise be infuriating.

3. Humor defuses tension and acts as a cathartic for negative emotions.

4. Humor acts as an emotion-focused strategy to change the perception of a stressful event and to decrease one's anxiety.

Case after case shows that humor improves morale in the elderly, decreases agitation and relieves lonely dissatisfaction.

When we add up all these benefits, it seems quite clear that humor can slow down aging, that it extends life, and that it will reverse the aging process.

In research carried out by the Laughter Project at the University of California at Santa Barbara, it was found that laughter did as well in reducing stress as more complex biofeedback training programs did.

Never before in history have there been so many people who have lived into their eighties, nineties, and hundreds.

"I'm making
old age
fashionable;
people can't wait
to get old."

— GEORGE BURNS, comedian,
at age 88

Modern medicine has helped add extra years to life but the "chronologically advantaged" know that one of the best ways to beat the clock is with a healthy dose of wit.

Here's a sample from the lips of an 88-year-old-woman in a Los Angeles residential care facility:

> *Three elderly men were sitting on a bench in Griffith Park.*
>
> *"When I die," said the first, "I hope it's in a hurry. I'd be satisfied to die in the crash of a speeding car,"*
>
> *"Nah!" disagreed the second. "I think it'd be better to die in a plane crash."*
>
> *"Well," said the third. "I'd rather die of smoke inhalation from blowing out one hundred candles on my birthday cake."*

I know I've said this before but it bears repeating. Laughter requires no special training, no special equipment and no special laboratory atmosphere. All it requires is a funny bone.

A kindly, sweet-faced 92-year old bachelor at a Pacific Grove retirement home made my day in relating his favorite story:

> *A married couple were celebrating their Sixtieth Wedding Anniversary. It was such a special newsworthy event the local TV station sent a crew to film an interview with them.*
>
> *"How old is your wife?" asked the news anchor.*

"And how old are you?" the anchor asked.

"I'm eighty-seven, too," he answered, "and God willing I'll live to be a hundred and one."

"But why," asked the reporter, "would you want to live one year longer than your wife?

"To tell you the truth," he replied, "I'd like to have at least one year of peace."

"The joyfulness of a man prolongeth his days."

— CHINESE PROVERB

135

In his book, *Ageless Body, Timeless Mind* Dr. Deepak Chopra lists some "Positive Factors that Retard Aging." Among them:

- Happy marriage
  (or satisfying long-term relationship).

- Job satisfaction.

- Feeling of personal happiness.

- **Ability to laugh easily.**

> **"Humor isn't for everyone. It's only for people who want to have fun, enjoy life and feel alive."**
>
> — ANN WILSON SCHAEF, author

Old age is reserved for very special people —
young people can't handle it.

A look at famous, active, still functioning
octogenarians reveals their positive outlook on life
and feeling young.

Have you ever noticed that so many comedians
seem to live longer?

A fellow spends his whole life just telling jokes
and lives to be one hundred years old — George
Burns.

> *Burns was being interviewed on his*
> *birthday. The reporter asked, "Can you*
> *still get out and walk around?"*
> *"Well," he replied, "I walk a lot better*
> *today than I did a hundred years ago."*

When George Burns celebrated his ninetieth
birthday he quipped,

> *"At my age it's nice to have birthday*
> *parties; all my friends can stand around*
> *the cake and keep warm."*

> *A fan once asked him, "What is the*
> *secret to a long life?"*
> *Burns replied, "Keep breathing."*

Lucille Ball was with us until she was 77,
Charlie Chaplin, 88. Among the entertainers
interviewed in my book, *The Great Comedians,*
Talke About Comedy, Jack Benny lived to be 80, so
did Ed Wynn. George Jessel, 83, Maurice Chevalier,
84, Jimmy Durante, 87.

And what about Red Skelton and Milton Berle
living into their late eighties? And Bob Hope into
his nineties?

A good sense of humor allows you to grow old gracefully. Some seniors have that wonderful gift for jesting about life.

Groucho Marx had a heart attack at age 84 and a doctor was called to the scene:

> *"Mr. Marx," said the M.D. "I'm going to take your temperature."*
> *"Where are you going to take it?" asked Groucho.*

Frank Sinatra showed his wit on the subject this way:

> *Somebody asked him what he wanted for his birthday and Sinatra replied, "Another birthday."*

And here's a typical senior displaying his sprightly sense of humor:

> *A reporter for the Arizona Republic newspaper in Phoenix, did an article on longevity. He interviewed an elderly resident living in Sun City, the famous retirement community. The man was married for 53 years.*
> *"Tell me, sir, what is the secret to a long happy marriage?"*
> *"Well, my wife and I like to go out to dinner twice a week," replied the old man. "A nice restaurant, candle-light, soft music, a good bottle of wine, then afterwards, a nice long walk home in the moonlight. She goes Tuesdays and I go Thursdays."*

"Time spent
laughing
is time
spent
with
the Gods."

—JAPANESE SAYING

DO YOU HAVE HUMOR DEFICIENCY SYNDROME?

Millions suffer from HDS. Take this test to see if you are aging gracefully. Simply answer TRUE or FALSE.

1. You wake up each morning complaining — too little sleep, too many aches and pains, another crummy day.

2. You drag yourself to the closet and find that your basic black wardrobe looks too bright.

3. You read the obituary page over breakfast and think, "Those lucky ducks."

4. Everybody on the road is a lousy driver except for you.

5. Everyone ahead of you in the express line line at the supermarket is conspiring to slow your progress.

6. Do you light up a whole room just by leaving it?

7. When playing cards, golf or tennis your blood boils when you don't beat the pants off your opponents.

8. It makes you feel better to regale family and friends with detailed accounts of your daily misfortunes.

9. Your favorite topics of dinner conversation are your backache, sore feet, food allergies and cholesterol readings.

10. If somebody teases you or makes a joke at your expense you react angrily and hold a grudge forever.

11. Daily chores — banking, laundry, errands, etc. — are an endless source of complaint.

12. You can't help ranting and raving about how society is deteriorating and how the country is going to hell in a handcart.

13. You find that talk radio and TV news are spiritually uplifting.

14. You feel overworked, underpaid and under appreciated.

15. It is your duty to criticize friends, co-workers and family members for their own good.

16. You think jokes are silly, offensive and a foolish waste of time.

17. When somebody beats you to a parking
spot, you secretly wish you had a
bazooka on board.

18. When someone tells you a joke you either
groan, or hasten to point out that it's not
funny or politically incorrect.

19. Cheerful people are annoying and you
suspect they're faking it — nobody
is *that* happy.

20. Anybody who does not share your
political or religious beliefs is an un-
informed, wrong-headed ignoramus.

RATE YOURSELF:

0-3 TRUE — You do not have a *Humor
Deficiency Syndrome*. In fact,
your sense of humor is your
greatest asset.

4-9 TRUE — You are showing the first signs of
Humor Deficiency Syndrome.
Make sure to get at least 15 good
laughs a day.

10-20 TRUE — An advanced case of HDS.
A funny bone transplant is your
only hope. On the bright side,
you will never die laughing.

SEVEN SIMPLE STRATEGIES TO UP YOUR DAILY HUMOR DOSE

You have to learn to exercise your innate ability to laugh because if you work at it you'll naturally see and feel more fun and enjoyment in life.

When you expose yourself to something funny every day you uncover your own formula for successful living — and love every minute of it.

Some tips:

1. Find out what makes you laugh.
   Then start your own humor library.

2. Practice laughing no matter how you feel at any given moment.

3. Hang out with people who laugh easily — it's contagious.

4. Find a laugh partner — someone who laughs at the same things you laugh at. A shared sense of humor will make good times better and the bad times less difficult.

5. Learn to laugh **with** others rather than laugh **at** them.

6. Watch the TV sitcoms and the comedians: David Letterman, Jay Leno, Garry Shandling, Rosie O'Donnell, and Conan O'Brien.

7. And most of all, look for the funny side of life.

Which just happens to be Step Five.

"The only thing
worth having
in an earthly
existence is a
sense of humor."

—LINCOLN STEFFENS,
journalist

Step Five

Look for
the
Funny Side
of Life

"If you ever
find happiness
by hunting for it,
you will find it,
as the old woman did
her lost spectacles,
safe on her own
nose all the time."

—JOSH BILLINGS,
humorist

*If you don't start out the day
with a smile, it's not too late to
start practicing for tomorrow.*

You Can Learn to
Find Humor Even in a Swamp
Full of Alligators

WHAT IS THERE IN LIFE THAT IS SO SERIOUS
we can't laugh at it?

A long standing comic equation goes:

Tragedy plus time equals comedy.

After a passage of time any event, no matter
how unfortunate or catastrophic, can yield to
humor. H.G. Wells, the English novelist and
historian wrote: "The crisis of today is the joke of
tomorrow."

When comedian Bill Cosby's son was murdered

147

"You can turn painful
situations around
through laughter.
If you can find humor
in anything
— even poverty —
you can survive it."

— BILL COSBY,
comedian

the entire nation shared his grief. An internationally known entertainer whose stock in trade is making people laugh. How would this man deal with a tragedy of such magnitude?

In the weeks following the murder he was interviewed on television. After expressing his sorrow and heartbreak he said, "I think it's time for me to tell the people that we have to laugh — we've got to laugh."

We desperately need to relieve the pain and anguish of our grief. The loss of a loved one may seem unendurable yet Cosby's words are an inspiring guide for the grieving. The only remedies to ease the loss are time, faith and laughter.

> "Life can be wildly
> tragic at times.
> But whatever
> happens to you,
> you have to keep a
> slightly comic attitude.
> In the final analysis,
> you have got not
> to forget to laugh."
>
> — KATHARINE HEPBURN,
> actor

IS THERE LAUGHTER AFTER DEATH?

Folks throughout the ages have found ways to smile in the face of life's most serious subject. No matter how sad or sorrowful death is, whether it's the passing of a beloved leader, friend or family member there is humor to be found.

Evidence this timeless story:

> A Wall Street broker passed away and the parish priest was delivering the eulogy before a large church gathering. "Frank Pettibone was a pillar of the community, generous to a fault, a wonderful father, a faithful husband and a true family man."
>
> Mrs. Pettibone tapped her son on the shoulder and said, "Go up and look in the box, make sure that's your father in there!"

"People use humour to lighten a seemingly awful burden. If you can laugh at a problem, its power over you has lessened."

—WENDY COPE,
British poet

150

TRAVAILS WITH MY AUNT

A lifetime in the "people business," has fostered my persistent pursuit of the understanding of human behavior. There's one fascinating characteristic that has become evident to me. I've observed that no matter how successful, famous or wealthy an individual becomes, the singularly most admirable trait that person can possess is a mirthful spirit — the ability to see the funny side of life and to bring that joy and humor to others.

The day Jack Benny lay dying in the bedroom of his Beverly Hills home, a small coterie gathered in the living room. Benny's manager, several of his writers and a bunch of his buddies were there. Instead of crying and mourning they were reminiscing, telling funny stories about Jack and laughing.

Down through the ages philosophers have taught us a thin line exists between comedy and tragedy. The same can be said for laughter and tears.

I consider myself very fortunate in having an aunt who taught me that it was just as easy to laugh as to cry. I was four years old, growing up in a third world country — *Joisey* City, New *Joisey.*

My father went bankrupt. He was a prodigious poker player who in time gambled away the car, the house and his business.

Yes, the same father who wouldn't allow his kids to squander nickels on the Coney Island merry-go-round and didn't believe in wasting money on play was in fact a big-time player .

We went on welfare. (It was called "relief" in those days.) And to ease the financial burden of raising four kids, my parents sent me to live in Belmar, New Jersey with my great aunt Bella.

She truly turned out to be a great aunt. She was a middle-aged woman, never married, yet she took to lovingly caring for her frightened four-year-old nephew, whom she nicknamed, "Sonny."

Living with her, I was treated to home-baked cakes and cookies, served with huge helpings of hugs and kisses and her undivided attention. But I was only four. I missed my mama. And I cried a lot.

Aunt Bella had an old, gray, moth-eaten fur hat with a plume on the back. When she put on the hat, it looked like a pregnant squirrel squatting on her head. It made me laugh.

The minute I'd start crying, she'd run in, put on the hat and I'd giggle. Then she spoke the words that would impact my entire life. She'd say, "See Sonny, it's just as easy to laugh as it is to cry."

I was four. She was fifty-four. For the next thirty years I had a love affair with a white-haired, blue-eyed, rosy-cheeked lady who became the symbol of everything that was good and kind in my world. When she died, I thought they were going to have to carry me away.

If success were measured by the gifts we give others, my Aunt Bella would be listed in everybody's *Who's Who*.

But her recipes for cinnamon-apple cake and ginger snap cookies aren't published in any cookbook. The sweaters she knitted for me with lumpy shoulders would never make the pages of *Gentlemen's Quarterly*. Her mark on the world is the gift of love she gave to me.

She taught me the value and the necessity of laughter. She also taught me to say "please" and "thank you," to open the door for a woman, to respect adults, to worship our God, and never, *never* to walk on the neighbor's lawn.

So many times since she died I've wished that I could repay her in some small way, hug her and kiss her and tell her how much I adored her.

But the day of her funeral I was flooded with vivid memories of my childhood with her. I could actually smell the wild honeysuckle she used to pick and see her hanging the sheets out in the backyard on a sunny day.

I recalled her soft hand taking me down to the corner grocery. Even though money was scarce, she always managed to find an extra couple of pennies to buy me an ice cream.

I heard her singing and laughing and remembered the tears she wiped away the day my parents finally came to take me home.

Then, in the midst of her funeral the full force of her influence over me came to bear. A vision of her in that funny, squirrelly hat flashed into my head and I did what she taught me. I started laughing. Joyfully. Gleefully. Uncontrollably.

Of course, there were startled glances from relatives and friends. They missed the joke.

But as I sat there chuckling, I heard her say just as clear as could be, "See Sonny, it's just as easy to laugh as it is to cry."

I don't know what people around me thought, but I know God forgave me. I was just sharing one last laugh with my sweet aunt Bella.

Years later I read the words by George Bernard Shaw which helped put my experience in perspective: "Life does not cease to be funny when people die, anymore than it ceases to be serious when people laugh."

To see the funny side of life, we've got to be able to laugh about everything — even death.

Woody Allen puts it this way: "I'm not afraid to die, I just don't want to be there when it happens."

"When I'm happy
I feel like crying,
but when I'm sad
I don't feel
like laughing.
I think its better
to be happy.
Then you get
two feelings for
the price of one."

— LILY TOMLIN,
comedian

Poking fun at the human condition has provided us with funny stories to fit every situation. Even death. Blasphemous? Perhaps. Necessary? Without a doubt. Witness:

The vice president of a bank in Texas passed away and his wife asked the minister to deliver the eulogy. "You can't be serious Mrs. Barnett. Everybody knows what a terrible person your husband was."

"Oh, Reverend, the entire family will be there," sobbed the widow. "I know that you'll find something nice to say."

The next day the minister said to the mourners. "We're gathered here today to pay our final respects to Howard Barnett. He wasn't a real nice fellow. He never supported his wife and family properly. He drank, gambled, ran around with other women. But compared to his brother Billy, he was an angel!"

"Humor is like a bulletproof vest that protects you against negative emotions."

—NORMAN COUSINS, author.

LAUGHTER: THE SPLENDID SPIRIT LIFTER

After a program I did for an Ohio company, attendees left the Cleveland hotel and I was collecting the materials used in my presentation.

As I headed for the entrance a man burst through the doors, spotted me, and rushed over.

"I was half way home," he began breathlessly, "but I just had to turn around and come back."

Then he told me his story.

"I heard you speak today and I wanted to tell you, I've been having a lot of problems with my teenage son. He's been using drugs. He's made our lives a living hell.

"The police arrested him three days ago for selling cocaine. I haven't been able to sleep. My wife is on the verge of a nervous breakdown. I came to hear you today because I needed a break from all this stress."

The man was clearly upset, yet there was spirit and a sparkle of hope in his eyes.

"When you talked about seeing the funny side of life and told those funny stories I began to relax. I started laughing, like never before. It was if a boulder had been lifted from my chest. For the first time in months I felt relief. I realize now how important it is not to lose your sense of humor."

HUMOR: THE MIRACULOUS MOOD ELEVATOR

I've seen humor work its miracles so many times. While waiting for a plane in Los Angeles, I noticed a young woman sitting across the way sobbing, her eyes red and swollen.

I wondered what tragedy had visited her life. A death in the family? The break-up of a marriage? Something had clearly broken her heart. Not wanting to intrude I noted her distress briefly and went back to reading my newspaper.

Fifteen minutes later, I looked up and she was gone. In a short time she returned. Evidently, she'd gone to the airport newsstand, for now she was clutching a joke book. My interest was immediately piqued —I recognized the colorful cover — it was my latest title.

An author doesn't generally get to see first-hand reaction to his work. This was my opportunity. I watched surreptitiously as she read, witnessing the stress gradually melt from her face like snow in summer. Soon she was smiling and chuckling.

It was the best book review I ever hope to get.

"When you're depressed,
the whole body
is depressed.
The first objective
is to get your
energy up,
and you can do it
through laughter.
It's one of the most
powerful ways of
breaking up
hopelessness."

—O. CARL SIMONTON, M.D.

SICK HUMOR SYNDROME

Health care professionals are notorious for finding laughter in what the rest of us might call sick humor. They encounter traumatic events that would make most of us buckle.

For many the key to surviving the blood, guts and mayhem is having an irreverent sense of humor. Even under battleground conditions the human spirit manages to preserve the ability to see things in a humorous way.

After a seminar for San Francisco's Mt. Zion Hospital residents, the doctors were eager to relate their favorite funny stories to me, and I pass them on to you:

An M.D. had just completed the operation and while washing up was joined by another young intern.

"Well, how did Mrs. Gardiner's appendectomy go?"

"Appendectomy?" shrieked the surgeon. "I thought it was an autopsy."

A fellow in a motorcycle accident lay in the hospital bed completely bandaged. His doctor appeared and with a smile said to him, "I've got good news and bad news,"

"What's the bad news?" he asked

"I'm sorry," said the M.D. "but I had to amputate both your feet."

"Oh, God!" sobbed the patient. "What's the good news?"

"The guy in the next bed wants to buy your boots."

*A Philadelphia internist had just
examined the x-rays of a close friend and
discovered he had an incurable cancer.
The physician turned to his nurse and
sobbed, "This is horrible. My oldest friend
and I have to tell him he's only got a
year to live. What a nightmare to have to
give him news like that."*

*"It's all right, doctor," said the
nurse, "I just told him."*

*"You told him!" wailed the M.D.,
"But I wanted to tell him."*

Among nurses there is a shared siege mentality
that exists in hospitals and clinics. This relentless
daily life-and-death struggle can cause depression
and emotional burnout. So privately, they often
joke about illness. What would appear to be a
twisted sense of humor to outsiders is their
psychological life preserver. By learning to see the
funny side of life nurses relieve the grave pressures
they face.

Each year the *Journal of Nursing Jocularity*
produces the "Humor Skills for Health
Professionals Conference" attended by hundreds of
RN's. Here are some of the typically irreverent
quips from conferees:

*What do you get when an epileptic
falls into the lettuce patch?
Seizure salad.*

*How does a leper end a poker game?
He throws in his hand.*

*What goes "ha ha ha thump"!
A leper laughing his head off!*

"The art of medicine
consists of amusing
the patient while
nature cures
the disease."

— VOLTAIRE,
French writer

What do they call the national organization of herpes sufferers? The American Lesion.

On a chart describing the frequency of the patient's vomiting, a student nurse wrote: "It comes and goes in spurts."

A man in his late seventies went back for his two week checkup. His doctor informed him there was good news and bad news.

"The bad news is you have the beginning stage of Alzheimer's. The good news is you can go home and forget about it."

Sick jokes can be shocking. Many are so bizarre we may wince before laughing uproariously. Sure, the gags are outrageous, insensitive and offensive, but they are also very human. For life itself can be outrageous, insensitive and offensive. But there is a deep human need to see the funny side of life no matter how tragic the circumstance.

Sick jokes were a fad in the Sixties. Comedian Lenny Bruce was described as "walking softly and carrying a big sick." Mort Sahl, Tom Lehrer, Shelley Berman, Dick Gregory and Bob Newhart were accused of using gags that smacked of morbidity and downright bad taste. But this type of humor was around long before these funny men helped make it a national craze.

In other times sick jokes were referred to as Cruel Jokes, Bloody Marys, Meanie Jokes, Depression Jokes, Hate Jokes, Sadist Jokes, Ivy League Jokes, Gruesomes, Grimsels and the

"Humor
is essential
for anyone in
health care.
It's the one thing
that makes the
workplace more
enjoyable and
keeps the
employees happy."

— DON MARQUIS,
cartoonist

Comedy of Horror.

No matter what they have been called, most sick jokes have in common the ridiculing of affliction. There is a seeming callous disregard for sentiment, tenderness, religious institutions or revered persons.

The jokes poke fun at mutilation, deformity and physical handicaps. The hunchback thus takes his place beside the moron and the loony as fodder for tickling the funny bone.

A century ago there were popular sick jokes called *Little Willies*. The term "getting the willies" — having a bad case of nerves or a feeling of uneasiness — prompted this form of humor.

Little Willies were short verses in couplet rhyme, first appearing in an English collection called *Ruthless Rhymes for Heartless Homes* by Harry Graham in 1899. They received instant popular acclaim and proliferated into thousands.

Some examples:

Willie, hitting at a ball
Lined one down the schoolhouse hall.
Through his door came Dr. Hill.
Several teeth are missing still.

Willie, as the fire burned low
Gave it a terrific blow.
Grandpa's beard got in the draft;
Dear me, how the firemen laughed!

Willie split the baby's head,
To see if brains were gray or red,
Mother, troubled, said to Father
"Children are an awful bother."

"Events in life
are not necessarily
good or bad.
It's our perspective.
Humor helps
us change
our perspective
of events."

— WALEED SALAMECH,
psychologist

Into the cistern little Willie
Pushed his little sister Lily.
Mother couldn't find our daughter
Now we sterilize our water.

In today's super sensitive, politically correct enviornment, these jokes could never catch on. Perhaps we have become more understanding and less spiteful toward our fellow beings.

"Hearty laughter
gives a sense of
deep relaxation
and tends to soften
our perspective
on problems.
It also eases pain."

— WAYNE PICKERING,
motivational nutritionist

A GOOD SENSE OF HUMOR LASTS

Seeing the funny side of life helps to relieve some of the pain. I know I've said that before but here's an incident that hits the point on the head.

Bob Hope had a long-time friendship with a vaudeville dancer named Barney Dean who Hope described in his book, *Don't Shoot, It's Only Me,* as the "sweetest, kindest, wittiest, most loyal friend a fellow ever had."

Dean did a dance act with another man. Barney described the team as "the slowest whirlwind dancers in show business." Hope kiddingly called Dean "the Jewish Fred Astaire."

At the beginning of Hope's career, the dancer raved about the new young comedian to theater bookers and Hope never forgot it. Years later Hope ran into him in Hollywood.

> *"Where've you been," Hope asked him. "What have you been doing?*
> *"Same old thing," Barney said. "Selling handcuffs."*

Hope and Bing Crosby hired Dean to hang out on the set of their "Road" pictures and he often came up with lines that were funnier than those written in the script. His witty ad-libs have become Hollywood lore:

> *Barney once got stopped for jaywalking in Beverly Hills and apologized, "I'm sorry, Officer. How fast was I going?"*

Dean worked for Hope until the day he died and what Dean said on his deathbed is the point I am aiming for.

Hope heard that Dean was dying and rushed to his room at Cedars of Lebanon Hospital. The ex-vaudevillian lay white-faced and weak in the bed knowing the end was near. Hope could see that his friend had little time left. Finally, Dean barely opened his eyes, looked up at Hope and said, "Anything you want me to tell Jolson?"

Funny right to the end.

> "Humor is emotional chaos remembered in tranquillity."
>
> —James Thurber, author

HUMOR BREAKS THE ICE AND
SMOOTHES COMMUNICATION

It's very often troublesome for people from a foreign country to appreciate American humor. Especially when they've grown up speaking a different language, and cultural lines must be crossed. However, some subjects are humorous in every culture and can be helpful in opening up friendly communication. There was an occasion once when it worked for me.

PEN is a literary organization, founded by William Wordsworth. PEN stands for Poets, Essayists and Novelists. Members include many famous and not-so-famous authors from around the world.

For a time, I served as president of the PEN Los Angeles Chapter. Part of my responsibility was to welcome members from foreign countries who were visiting California.

One evening, two Taiwanese authors and their wives joined my wife and me, and the PEN vice-president and her husband for dinner.

The Asians were rather shy. We chatted politely but it was quite obvious that they felt a little uneasy.

Our cordial conversation centered around writing, their impressions of the United States and the weather.

As dinner progressed our foreign guests continued to appear ill-at-ease. When the subject of marriage came up the PEN V.P. explained that she and her husband just celebrated their 32nd anniversary.

The Taiwanese wives seemed to enjoy hearing that information, which reminded me of a funny story about marriage, one I thought would be appropriate and that might make our visitors feel at ease. I worried momentarily that they might not laugh, that even though they were educated writers and spoke English, perhaps the humor wouldn't cross cultural lines. But I decided to take the risk. So I told this story:

> When the California earthquake hit our home I was upstairs in the office. My wife was downstairs in the kitchen. Pictures fell off the walls and crashed to the floor. The stairs began to shake as I rushed down and called to my wife. She joined me in the front doorway and we clung to each other for dear life.
>
> The building rocked back and forth. We held each other tightly, as the swaying motion moved us back and forth, up and down, around and around. When the movement finally stopped my wife began to sob.
>
> "Don't cry," I said, "We're not hurt. We're alive! We can repair all the damage."
>
> "It's not that," she sniffled. "Do you realize this is the first time since we got married that we've been out dancing?"

If you're planning a trip to Taiwan, let me know. I'd like to introduce you to some friends there who love the American sense of humor.

"If you wish to glimpse
inside a man,
don't bother analyzing
his ways of talking,
of weeping, of seeing
how much he is
moved by noble ideas;
you will get
better results
if you just watch
him laugh.
If he laughs well,
he is a good man."

— FYODOR DOSTOYEVSKI,
Russian author

LAUGHING YOUR ALLIGATORS IN THE FACE

In some ways, this strategy epitomizes the essential message of this book. To achieve inner peace, to find some semblance of happiness, we've got to be able to laugh at the tricks life plays on us. As we get older we have a choice. Either we can laugh, or we can cry.

A *Time* magazine feature article concerning the latest research on prostate trouble (of which I have personal and intimate interest) noted that it is a disease usually afflicting men over the age of forty.

You know what prostate trouble is. That's when men begin stuttering from the wrong end.

In basketball parlance it's known as the "double dribble."

The leak a plumber cannot fix.

The *Time* article reminded me of a drive my wife I took to San Francisco recently.

The trip from our home usually takes around three hours. But last time it took five hours and fifty-five minutes.

Why?

My version of "Oh, Susanna," will explain:

> *My wife and I went on a trip*
> *For things we had to buy;*
> *It took the whole darn day to drive*
> *And here's the reason why:*
> *It's my prostate,*
> *It needs an overhaul.*
> *I had to stop and run like hell*
> *To answer nature's call.*

I peed all night the day we left
My bladder it was dry.
But soon I had to go again;
It made me wanna cry.
Oh, my prostate
No matter where I roam
It makes no difference where I am
The toilet is my home.

When raindrops fall I have to go
A drizzle drives me wild
I make so many potty stops
You'd think I was a child.
Oh, my prostate,
It's difficult to lust
My age is catching up with me
My plumbing's full of rust.

The toughest time to see the funny side of life is when bad things affect us personally — when we're up to our eyeballs in alligators. And yet, this is precisely the time when we need humor the most.

"I give them
something to
laugh at.
Then while their
mouths are open
I give them
something to
chew on."

— BILLY GRAHAM.
minister

Summing Up

"The comic spirit
is given to us
in order that
we may analyze,
weigh and
clarify things
which nettle us."

— THORNTON WILDER,
novelist, playwright

*A smile is a light on
your face to let people
know you are home.*

Summing Up

IT'S QUITE CLEAR THAT AN APPRECIATION OF
humor can be learned, it's an intuitive intelligence
that can be nourished and improved.

Television writer Gene Perret says, "Humor is
an attitude. It's a way of looking at life and of telling
others how you feel about what's happening
around you."

Humor shows us the absurdity of life's
absurdities. It becomes abundantly apparent that
there are very few things in life that do not have a
humorous side. It allows us to turn painful
experiences into hilarious escapades.

And humor is accessible to everyone. You don't
need a Harvard degree to reap the benefits. You

don't even need money. It simply requires a change in your point of view.

We're the only species on this earth that has the capacity on one hand to totally destroy this globe, and, yet on the other, has the ability to laugh.

It's up to each of us to make sure that joy and laughter are never outweighed by tragedy.

Living life with a mirthful perspective, a jolly disposition, requires daily exercise and constantly trying to do more. We've all got to keep reminding ourselves of the fundamentals: laughing out loud; laughing at our own foibles; smiling through adversity; incorporating humor into our daily lives; and looking for that humorous ray of sunshine even in the midst of trauma and tragedy.

No one has ever achieved success in any endeavor without effort and awareness.

But we can improve our attitudes of mind and move to a new level for happier, healthier living.

Of course we must practice. The rewards are clear, immediate and abundant. Laughter is a miracle drug, a remedy that eases pain, cures depression, and helps us put our lives into manageable perspective.

When we banish tension, fear and worry with laughter, we free our minds to focus on the solutions.

Humor makes us look at life a little differently than we have. It helps to turn pain inside out and render it powerless to defeat us.

In summing up, I feel it's appropriate to remind you once again that laughter is universal. It crosses all boundries. It transcends language, race, color, creed, custom, religion, age, the rich or poor. Laughter softens the edges of a harsh world.

Perhaps the best way to sum it all up is with the wonderfully wise words of the great American humorist, Will Rogers: "We're all here for just a short spell — get all the good laughs you can."

He who laughs,
lasts.

— A. NON YMOUS

Ten Commandments
for Lighthearted Living
(Okay, Eleven)

I.   Make up your mind that no
matter what happens you're
going to be a happy person.
If you're not having fun,
FAKE IT.

II.   Start the day with a smile
by reading something funny.
Skip the stress of listening
to the news.

III.   If you meet someone who
hasn't got a smile, give
them yours.

IV.   Keep a clip file of cartoons and
jokes handy for emergency
infusions of humor.

V.   Laugh at your troubles. Crying
      is no fun and complaining
      does no good.

VI.   Laugh at your dumb
      mistakes before others
      have a chance to.

VII. Laugh with your spouse and
      your marriage will improve
      with age.

VIII. Laugh with your kids and
      they'll never stop loving you.

IX.   Don't laugh with your
      relatives — it will encourage
      them to borrow money.

X.   Keep smiling! It makes people
      wonder what you've been up to.

XI.   Remember: Angels fly because
      they take themselves lightly.

"Most folks
are about
as happy as
they make up
their minds to be."

— A. LINCOLN,
16th president

Humor 101

"Jokes of the
proper kind,
properly told, can do
more to enlighten
questions of
politics, philosophy,
and literature than
any number of
dull arguments."

— ISAAC ASIMOV,
author

*Humor is the sugar
that makes the
medicine go down.*

A Short Primer in the
Nuts and Bolts
of Comedy

ONE OF THE BEST WAYS TO INCORPORATE laughter into your life is to broaden your awareness of the humor around you and to develop a deeper understanding of what makes you laugh.

With that in mind, here is a basic course on humor appreciation. Everything you never knew you needed to know and may have been too depressed to ask.

If we wanted to know more about fine wines, classical music or modern art we'd read books or take some classes. Education is the key to broadening our grasp of any subject. And humor is no exception.

It's been said that there are two things one doesn't want to see in the making: sausages and jokes.

At the risk of exposing too much of the inner workings of humor and thereby spoiling the fun, we can nevertheless benefit from a little knowledge. In this case it's not a dangerous thing.

Ever wondered about the difference between an anecdote, joke and a funny story?

A one-liner and a riddle?

How professionals turn an amusing idea into a funny joke?

Read on. Here are the accepted forms most used to stimulate laughter.

Humor 101 is now in session.

In order to have a keener comprehension of humor the first area we must address are the basics for evoking laughter. As anyone who's ever given a successful speech knows, using humor is essential.

FIVE REASONS WHY PRESENTERS (if they're smart) RELY ON HUMOR

1. It's an icebreaker.

2. It captures attention.

3. It helps to drive home a point.

4. It entertains the audience.

5. Best of all, laughter keeps the audience from yawning.

Pete Peterson, a Wall Street financier who is in great demand as a speaker, says, "People never play back to me the serious remarks I make, they always remember some bit of humor I use to dramatize a point."

He's developed the Peterson Principle: "If you want anything to stick to the bone, use some humor that is relevant to your message."

But which kind of humor to use? It comes in many forms: anecdotes, riddles, one-liners, jokes and funny stories.

> "Jokes are
> mind-to-mind
> resuscitation."
>
> — John Lahr,
> author

ANECDOTES

These are short colorful accounts of true or seemingly true incidents that are entertaining, interesting or amusing.

Anecdotes are stories that can be told by almost everyone. And usually are.

"What Happened When I Drove Away From the Dealer In My New Car..."

"How I Met My Spouse..."

"The Night the Water Heater Broke..."

Garrison Keillor, Charles Osgood, Dave Barry and Calvin Trillin are among the masters at taking seemingly simple anecdotal incidents and stretching them into hilarious accounts.

The short stories of S.J. Perelman, Dorothy Parker, James Thurber, E.B. White and Robert Benchley are excellent examples of turning an apparently innocuous happening into an uproariously funny situation.

In professional speaking, humorists Doc Blakely, Robert Henry, Al Walker, Grady Jim Robinson and Jeanne Robertson are among the most gifted in evoking belly laughs from personal experiences.

Anecdotal humor is generally more effective when it is written rather than spoken.* When anecdotes are told in social situations they can be expected to produce only smiles or chuckles.

It's much easier to stimulate laughter with other forms of humor such as the riddle.

*See Travails With My Aunt page 151.

188

RIDDLES

These are perplexing or puzzling questions posed as problems to be solved or guessed and very often played as a game .

Children love riddles. It gives them an opportunity to ask a question, then provide a funny answer. This, of course, allows them to be the center of attention. They also feel clever and superior being able to supply the punch line.

Why don't cannibals eat clowns?
Because they taste funny.

What did the bald man say when
he got a comb for his birthday?
Thanks very much. I'll never part
with it.

What is the best thing to take
when you're run down?
The license number of the car that
hit you.

But riddles aren't just for kids. In some circles they might be considered silly or corny, however, being a grownup doesn't preclude your enjoying the fun.

What is a committee?
A life form with six or more legs and
no brains.

In what way does a lawyer resemble
a pelican?
In the length of his bill.

What do they call a 1956 Buick in Mississippi?
The bridal suite.

> "A joke is a trick
> you play on the
> listener's mind.
> You start him
> off toward a
> plausible goal...
> then by a sudden twist
> you land him
> just where he
> didn't expect to go."
>
> — MAX EASTMAN,
> author

ONE-LINERS

They are witty or clever comments usually expressed in one or two sentences.

This is the chief comic form used by most comedians and in sitcoms. The term encompasses quips, quotes, gaglines, and comic definitions. Some consider it the quintessential form of verbal humor in that a complete comedic thought is expressed in the fewest words.

The craft of creating one-liners is probably the singularly most difficult comic form to write. All aspects of the quip must be packed into one sentence. A highly respected trade in Hollywood, talented creators of good one-liners are in great demand.

The one-liner is favored by many performers. Because of television's influence, audiences today have a brief attention span. One-liners are short, easy to grasp, and quick to deliver laughs.

Billy Crystal, Robin Williams, Jerry Seinfeld, George Carlin, Eddie Murphy and Roseanne all depend on the one-liner.

Their predecessors, Bob Hope, Milton Berle and Henny Youngman built lifelong careers on these quick quips.

Henny Youngman's one-liners might be considered insensitive and politically uncouth today but they represent perfect examples of a funny thought being expressed in the fewest words:

Take my wife, please!

I take my wife everywhere but she always finds her way home.

Valentine's Day she gave me the
usual gift — she ate my heart out.

And some brilliant baubles from master craftsman, Woody Allen:

I don't believe in after-life,
although I am bringing along a change
of underwear.

I failed to make the chess team on
account of my height.

A stockbroker is someone who
invests other people's money until it's
all gone.

Amazingly, the following timeless twitters were penned more than sixty years ago by the great humorist, Will Rogers:

With Congress, every time they
make a joke it's a law. And every time
they make a law it's a joke.

I might have gone to West Point
but I was too proud to talk to a
congressman.

A bunch of American tourists were
hissed and stoned in France, but not
until they had finished buying.

There are only a few original
jokes, and most of them are in
Congress.

"If there is no malice
in your heart,
there can't be none
in your jokes."

—WILL ROGERS,
humorist

"My way of joking
is to tell the truth.
It's the funniest joke
in the world."

— GEORGE BERNARD SHAW,
British playwright,
novelist and critic

JOKES

Perhaps the most familiar form of comedic expression is the joke. It's usually short, simple to remember and easy to tell.

A quintessential definition is offered by Evan Esar, the esteemed humor historian, in *The Humor of Humor*: "A brief comic incident, stripped of all nonessential details. It begins with a situation, has no middle, and ends with a surprising or unexpected outcome."

The consummate joke format, is short and sweet:

After the physical examination Bigelow put on all his clothes and sat down at the doctor's desk.

When the M.D. finished speaking to his stockbroker on the phone he gave the patient a big smile. "Now I'm ready for you."

"Tell me the truth!" said Bigelow sorrowfully. "Am I going to get well?"

"Of course you are!" said the physician. "You're going to get well if it costs every cent you've got."

Keegan and Walker were discussing a mutual acquaintance. "He use to do work for me," said Keegan. "I wouldn't trust him with your money. He'd lie, steal, cheat, anything for a buck."

"How do you know him so well? asked Walker.

"How? I taught him everything he knows!"

Richard, age 10, walked into the men's room of an Orlando restaurant and looked at all the feet that showed beneath the cubicle doors.

After checking every stall, he approached one, knocked on it, and whispered, "Mom says you can come out now. Grandpa just paid the check."

> "The funniest
> joke of all
> is the absolute truth
> stated simply
> and gracefully."
>
> — CARL REINER,
> actor, writer, director

FUNNY STORIES

Funny stories have the same basic elements as jokes except that they are longer, have a beginning, middle and an end. The characters are also better defined.

Malcolm and Lucinda had been loving friends for many years. One day they were killed in an automobile accident and wound up in heaven.

They stood before St. Peter holding hands and said, "We would like to get married."

"Take your time, no need to rush," said St. Peter. "You've got an eternity to think about it. Come back and see me in fifty years."

Five decades later, the couple returned and once again informed St. Peter that they wanted to marry.

"Think about it some more. Come back again in another fifty years and if we don't have a preacher up here by then, I'll marry you myself."

One evening at dinner little Karla confided to her Dad that a boy in her kindergarten class asked her to play doctor with him.

Her father dropped his fork in shock. Calmly he asked, "And did you?"

"Yes, I did," answered Karla.

"Tell me everything he did," said the worried father.

"Well, first he kept me waiting for 45

minutes," she said, "then he doubled the bill for the insurance company."

A Coast Guard cutter was patrolling the waters off the California coast. Just after midnight it received a faint distress signal from a pleasure craft.

The radio operator responded immediately: "What is your position?" he shouted. "Repeat. What is your position?"

After several seconds of silence a voice came over the static, "I'm the vice president of Santa Barbara Insurance , Real Estate and Stock Brokers Limited — but could you please hurry!"

"A good joke
beats a pill
for a lot
of ailments"

— EMERY STYRON,
Editor, Mt. Pleasant News

> "Were it not for
> my little jokes,
> I could not bear
> the burdens
> of this office."
>
> — ABRAHAM LINCOLN,
> 16th president

Riddles, one-liners, jokes and funny stories are the most popular forms of verbal wit. They are often put to use by speakers, humorists, politicians, the clergy — all who appear before the public.

But other humor forms — the limerick and the pun — are seldom used to entertain an audience. They are deadly in the hands of the inexperienced and often explode in the face of the presenter.

"Hanging is too
good for a man
who makes puns;
he should be drawn
and quoted."

— FRED ALLEN,
comedian

PUNS

A pun is a humorous use of a word or words that sound alike but have two different meanings.

Kansas City is trying for more tourists because Missouri loves company.

Alimony is billing without the cooing.

Show me a man who's afraid of Christmas and I'll show you a Noel Coward.

Of all the many elements of humor, the pun has never gained great popularity in the gag genre. It has alternately been described as, "The lowest form of wit — among the witless."

And: "A form of humor that goes over with a groan.

Yet it still enjoys a wide and devoted following by all those with a well-developed, sophisticated sense of humor.

While puns can be a delightful source of amusement to the casual humor lover, most performers and speakers avoid them, chiefly because they elicit the "wrong" kind of laughter from an audience. Mostly groans.

Performers and speakers can never count on audience reaction. But the risk is even greater when using puns. Odds are a crowd will react negatively.

However, after a lifetime in the business of making people laugh I've come to love puns. They're fun, they tickle my funny bone, and they're great at a dinner party or social gathering. But I've

"A pun
is the lowest
form of humor —
when you
didn't think
of it first."

—OSCAR LEVANT,
pianist, composer

made it a point never to use one from the speaker's platform.

People have different tastes in humor. And that's the main reason it's practically impossible to get everyone in an audience to laugh at the same time at the same funny remark.

For those who fancy the subtle cleverness and wit of puns, here are two classics that have survived the test of time and a million moans and groans (and belly laughs):

The Hunchback of Notre Dame wanted to go on vacation so he put an ad in the paper for a temporary replacement. The next day an armless man showed up for the job.

"How you gonna ring the bell without any arms?" asked the Hunchback.

"I can do it with my face," replied the temp.

"I don't believe it," said the Hunchback, "but go ahead."

The armless man ran toward the bell and hit it with his face. The bell swung all the way out but when it returned it hit him and knocked him out of the church tower all the way to the ground.

The Hunchback rushed down the stairs and when he arrived on the street a crowd had gathered around the fallen Frenchman.

A gendarme tapped the Hunchback on the shoulder and asked, "Do you know this man?"

"No," he replied, "but his face sure rings a bell."

So good, there's even a sequel:

The next day another temp answered the Hunchback's ad. He too had no arms but was given a chance to ring the bell.

The Frenchman hit the bell, it swung out and when it came back it knocked him over the church tower wall and he landed twenty stories below.

When the Hunchback arrived a large crowd stood staring at the lifeless man.

"Do you know him?" asked a policeman of the Hunchback.

"No," said the Hunchback, "but he's a dead ringer for the first guy!"

> **"A laugh is worth
> a hundred groans
> in any market."**
>
> — CHARLES LAMB,
> English essayist and critic

A little nonsense
now and then,
Is relished by
the wisest of men.

— A. NON YMOUS

LIMERICKS

Limericks are humorous or nonsensical verses consisting of five lines that usually rhyme, making them easy to remember.

Limericks are the most favored of verse forms, and are created to express a funny thought.

Edward Lear is recognized as the godfather of the limerick because his first book, published in 1846, contained 112 examples and popularized the form.

What the nursery rhyme is to children, the limerick is to adults. Most are sophisticated, satirical and bawdy.

This special type of humor is rarely used by speakers and performers for three reasons:

1. Many people are not familiar with the form.

2. Others find them too subtle.

3. And, unfortunately, most of the funniest limericks are rude, risqué or obscene — certainly not suited for telling before a mixed audience.

However, told spiritedly in private or in the company of good friends, the limerick can be a sheer and total delight.

Some favorites:

> *The limerick packs laughs anatomical*
> *Into space that is quite economical.*
> *But the good ones I've seen*
> *So seldom are clean*
> *And the clean ones so seldom are comical.*

A bather whose clothing was strewed
By winds that left her quite nude,
Saw a man come along,
And unless I am wrong,
You expected this line to be lewd.

Finally, to end this delightful madness here's a limerick that even includes a pun:

There was a young man named Paul
Who fell in the spring in the fall
T'would have been a sad thing
If he died in the spring
But he didn't — he died in the fall.

There you have it. The short primer on the nuts and bolts of basic comedy. These have been the commonly accepted forms most used to stimulate laughter.

Whether your object is to perfect comic delivery for a speech or presentation, lighten the workplace or just improve the quality of your life, having a better understanding of humor spades the ground for a fertile crop of laughter.

Whatever you're trying to sell — a product, a service, yourself, — these fundamental forms, when used properly, will get positive results.

How, when, and where to use them is the subject of the next chapter.

"Forgive, oh, Lord,
my little jokes on thee
and I'll forgive thy
great big one on me."

— ROBERT FROST,
poet

When It's Laughter You're After

"I doubt there
is among us a more
useful citizen than the
one who holds the secret
of banishing gloom,
of making tears
give way to laughter,
of supplanting
desolation and despair
with hope and courage,
for hope and courage
always go with
a light heart."

— FRANKLIN D. ROOSEVELT,
33rd president

*If you'd like to spoil
the day for a grouch,
give him a smile.*

You Can Learn
How to be Funnier

CONDUCTING WORKSHOPS FOR EXECUTIVES
and coaching professional speakers and comedians
has taught me that the basic skills for being funny
apply to everybody.

For those who want to tell a joke at the water
cooler, relate a story at a dinner party or start a
business meeting with a bang there are really seven
basic laws for getting laughs.

Is it possible to perfect the skills required to
elicit laughter every time?

Can self-conscious joke-tellers acquire techniques to garner bigger, better laughs?

211

The answer is yes. Joke-telling can be cultivated.

Whether you're a professional presenter, politician, business leader, corporate executive, a member of the clergy or simply a humor aficionado, you can polish your presentation skills by merely practicing seven simple laws.

Larry's Law No. 1:

MEMORIZE THE PUNCH LINE FIRST

Nothing is more frustrating or disappointing for the listener than hearing someone starting to tell a funny story who suddenly blurts out, "Oh, damn, I forgot the punch line!"

In case you haven't noticed, the punch line is *the* most crucial element of the story. It's the line that ties the entire story together, makes the point, and delivers the payoff. Without it there is no laughter.

The rest of the story can be changed or twisted, adapted to fit different occasions or circumstances. But the punch line must not be changed. Once you learn it and can say it comfortably, the punch line must remain constant.

By memorizing the exact punch line word for word — no matter how poorly the initial part of the joke is told — you as the presenter can now relax. You can feel secure in knowing the punch line will be delivered correctly.

One of my closest show business friends loves hearing and telling the latest jokes. When I tell him a story he laughs at it and enjoys it but while he's laughing he repeats the punch line. When he stops laughing, he delivers the punch line aloud. Then he says, "That's funny!" and repeats the punch line one more time.

It took me awhile to figure out why he was repeating the punch line so many times. He was using a tried and true technique of memorization to add the story to his own repertoire.

Repeat the punch line often enough, it's yours forever.

That's why I recommend that when you read or hear a joke you like well enough to tell, learn the punch line **first**.

Repeat it out loud three times. Then do it again. Repetition is the key. Say it aloud while taking a shower or driving to work. Once you've learned it, can say it over and over without the slightest hesitation or floundering you can then learn the rest of the joke.

By memorizing the punch line first, getting it down letter perfect, you'll never spoil the chance to earn a good laugh by hesitating, stumbling, recalling or apologizing.

> **"Security
> is knowing
> your lines."**
>
> — MILTON BERLE,
> comedian

"People can
never resist those who
make them laugh."

—W. SOMERSET MAUGHAM,
author

Larry's Law No. 2

MINCE WORDS

Always tell a story in the fewest words possible.
Nothing stands in the way of a big laugh more than a joke that is wordier than necessary. The fewer the words the bigger the laugh. The size of the laugh is inversely proportional to the number of words used to reach the punch line.

Cutting excess verbiage is the mark of a true professional. When telling stories, more words are not better. *Less* is more.

Amateurs immediately communicate their lack of skill by unnecessarily stretching and embellishing a funny story.

Great storytellers spin yarns without using one extra word. They become great because they learn early on the inviolate rule:

> Most stories depend on concise
> wording to be funny.

The ability to ruthlessly edit one's words shows respect for the listener as well as a keen understanding of the art of communication.

Interviewing Jack Benny for *The Great Comedians Talk About Comedy*, I asked his secret for having such a long successful career. This is what he said: "I've always had good shows but I was almost a better editor. Most comedians give me credit for being not the best comedian in show business but the best editor ... which is as important as being a comedian. There is nothing as important as editing."

215

An example of sharp editing:

A divorced father had been hauled into court for non-payment of child support. On the witness stand, he cried, "As God is my judge, I do not owe the money."
The judge replied, "He's not. I am. You do."

All professional presenters — trainers, seminar leaders, keynote speakers — have learned one reliable technique to communicate effectively with an audience: validate your point with a colorful, memorable story, and do it succinctly.

> **"The wit of brevity lies in saying much in few words. With quips, as with other types of wit, the tighter, the brighter."**
>
> **— EVAN ESAR,**
> humor historian

This old folk tale is a case for verbal economy:

Once upon a time there was an island called Brevity where the natives hated people who talked too much. The inhabitants of Brevity said what they had to say in as few words as possible and expected everyone else to do the same.

Nearby there was an island called OnTooLong. One year famine struck On TooLong and the people sent Prince Babbler to ask for help. Babbler arrived on Brevity and launched into a description of the terrible famine, the suffering of the people, and how devastating the disaster would be for all the nearby islands.

Babbler rambled on for two hours and many of the Brevity delegation fell asleep. When Babbler finally finished, the Brevity Governor said, "I can't remember the beginning of your speech and I'm still hazy about the details that followed."

They sent Babbler back empty-handed. The people of OnTooLong sent another emissary, Dr. ShortTalk, urging him to be brief as possible requesting aid.

ShortTalk stood before the governing body of Brevity, holding empty rice bags. He spoke only three sentences. "My people are starving. These bags're empty. Please fill them." And he sat down.

The Governor of Brevity ordered the bags filled at once. Then he took the envoy aside and said, "There was no need to point out that the bags were empty. We saw that. And it wasn't necessary to ask to fill them. We would have done it anyway. If you come again, remember, don't talk so much."

After a keynote speaker had overstayed his allotted time on the platform by a full forty minutes, a sore-bottomed but silver-tongued program chairman consoled disgruntled members of the audience with this reminder:

It's never so bleak
But it could be bleaker,
There might have been
A second speaker!

Then he added these lines:

Charm and wit and levity
May help you at the start;
But in the end it's brevity
That wins the public's heart.

Why should one be dilligent in the quest for crispness in speech from the platform?

It's a mark of respect for the audience.

The most damning revelation you can make about yourself is that you don't know a clever and concise way to express what you want to say.

Unskilled presenters may not be aware that they are taking too long to get to the point or punch line.

The best way to avoid wordiness?

Choose your story.

Get down the salient points.

Then weed out verbiage by making sure that every word is vital to the story. If it's not, cut.

Cut. Cut. Cut.

Make it short and sweet.

No joke ever got funnier by getting longer.

"Be amusing;
never tell
unkind stories;
above all
never tell
long ones."

— BENJAMIN DISRAELI,
British Prime Minister

Larry's Law No. 3

REHEARSE. REPEAT. REHEARSE.

You can only tell a story well when it becomes second nature, and it will only become second nature with practice. Rehearse the story until it flows smoothly.

Only with practice can you achieve a flawless delivery.

Only with practice can you avoid the embarrassment of forgetting the punch line, or the moans of disappointment when you've left out the salient points.

This simple strategy will make you feel confident. Surely, that feeling of security is worthy of a little practice.

Repeat the entire story aloud in privacy.

Repeat it until you can tell it without the slightest mistake.

If you are serious about perfecting your skills, deliver the story into a tape recorder. Listen to it objectively.

Have you told it in the least number of words?

If not, edit the unnecessary, flowery sentences. Keep only the main points.

Then rehearse, rehearse, rehearse.

Tell the joke to everyone you meet. Your mother-in-law, the grocery clerk, an uncle, your bank teller, co-workers, the telephone operator. Anybody who will listen.

It's like the vintage joke:

A visitor to New York walked up to a newspaper stand and said to the dealer, "How do I get to Carnegie Hall?" "Practice, mister, practice!"

"Brevity
is the soul
of wit."

—WILLIAM SHAKESPEARE,
playwright

Larry's Law No. 4

DON'T LAUGH AT YOUR OWN JOKES

It's the same as applauding for yourself.

It indicates that you are insecure about the funniness of the material and are trying to help it along.

If you've rehearsed the story and are satisfied that you're telling it in the least number of words possible, your audience should laugh. If they don't, and your story doesn't get the reaction you'd hoped for, get rid of it. Time to try another story. The fun and challenge of telling humor well is finding material that suits your style.

Keep trying until you find the right joke that gets the kind of laugh you want. Then let the audience enjoy it.

Your mission is to tell the story so the audience can derive pleasure from it.

> **"I don't care how much a man talks, if he only says it in a few words."**
>
> **—JOSH BILLINGS,**
> **humorist**

> "I love a finished speaker,
> I really, truly do.
> I don't mean one who's polished,
> I just mean one who's through."
>
> —RICHARD ARMOUR,
> poet

Larry's Law No. 5

DON'T BLAME THE AUDIENCE IF IT DOESN'T RESPOND

If the audience doesn't react it's a good bet that the fault lies with the presenter.

Ask yourself:

Did you memorize the exact punch line?

Did you tell the story in the least number of words?

Did you practice telling the story until it became second nature?

Did you risk using a pun or limerick to get the laugh?

If you're still unsure of what happened, maybe you told the wrong joke at the wrong time.

It's critical to get the right kind of laugh. A shock laugh usually follows an off-color story. An embarrassed giggle almost always comes from the telling of a tasteless joke. Learn to judge the quality of your response.

Using four letter words for shock value is ill-advised in most circumstances. A good presenter knows the audience, is sensitive to its feelings and doesn't need to resort to vulgarity.

Finding suitable stories and telling them at the proper time and place is an acquired awareness. Expertise such as this can only be learned by trial and error.

These days audiences are more sensitive. Getting big laughs has become a greater challenge. It's possible but the jokes must be chosen with considerable care and effort. Today's successful presenter abstains from humor that could be conceived as sexist, ethnic or offensive.

The old joke goes:

Two fellows meet on the street and one says, "Who was that lady I saw you with last night?"

The other man says, "That was no lady that was my wife."

In today's politically correct super-sensitive environment that joke becomes:

Two persons of indeterminate gender meet on the street.

One says, "Who was that person of the same or opposite gender according to your sexual preference that I observed you with last night?"

The other one says, "That was no person of the same or opposite gender according to my sexual preference. That was my significant other."

I recommend avoiding both versions. Finding humor that works for you can be daunting. Keep experimenting.

> "There is nothing
> in the world
> like making
> people laugh."
>
> —CAROL BURNETT,
> comedian

Larry's Law No. 6

PERSONALIZE YOUR HUMOR

Your material will evoke louder and longer laughter if it has a ring of truth, if it sounds believable. Listeners want to give credence to what you say.

When cowboys crowded around a campfire they were enthralled by the storyteller recounting tales of bygone days, painting word pictures that aroused the imagination. He lifted spirits. His listeners hung on every word. He held his audience in the palm of his hand because his yarns sounded believable whether they were true or not.

Your story must sound like the truth. It doesn't have to be real but it must *seem* to be true. Very few stories are retold exactly the way they happened. They are embellished and often exaggerated for comedic purposes. But the more truthful the story sounds the more your listeners will get caught up in what you say.

One sure way to do this, is to make yourself an integral part of the story:

This morning my wife reminded me...

Let me tell you what happened to me last week as I was coming back from ...

My uncle just went on a cruise down to the Caribbean and he told me about this couple on the ship who ...

You won't believe what I saw today at the supermarket ...

"So important is
laughter
that societies
highly reward
those who make
a living by inducing
laughter in others."

— STEVE ALLEN,
comedian

Larry's Law No. 7:

MAKE SURE THE AUDIENCE UNDERSTANDS EVERY WORD

Listeners can't laugh if they can't understand what you are saying.

Speak clearly and distinctly. Slur a key word and the joke is lost.

Another thing that can destroy audience response is improper use of the microphone. This is deadly.

Not long ago, an attractive young woman was showcased at a "Professional Speakers Association" chapter meeting that I attended. She used a hand-held mike.

She was pleasant, had an interesting topic and possessed a lively sense of humor. Throughout her talk, she moved her head left and right to gain direct eye contact with the audience. This is an excellent technique to communicate and develop a strong rapport with your audience.

Unfortunately, when she turned her head she neglected to move the hand-held microphone in the same direction. Most of the audience missed what she was saying. Several funny stories were ruined. We saw her mouthing the words but without the mike, we lost elements vital to the punch lines. Reaction? A sprinkling of laughter, mostly sympathetic.

Proper mike training and practice could turn her talk into something special. But without it, she's just another wannabe.

Whether you're a professional or simply telling a joke to a co-worker at the water cooler and your object is to get a laugh, don't diminish the laugh by garbling your words.

Clear, concise speech is essential for communication. Are you as surprised as I am that in this high tech age there are so many people who leave messages on answering machines that are indecipherable?

> "Next to being
> witty yourself,
> the best thing is
> being able to
> quote another's wit."
>
> — EVAN ESAR,
> humor historian

A NOTE TO PROS

While this book is aimed at everyone who wants to have a greater appreciation of humor, the following pointers are directed at those who are (or want to be) pros.

- **Failure to prepare is preparation for failure.**

  I don't know who wrote that but I live by it. No amount of effort is too great in order to achieve success from the platform. Especially if we are being paid. We have an artistic responsibility to the client, the audience and to ourselves to be the best we can possibly be. Impeccable preparation insures that goal.

- **Don't over gesticulate.**

  Using exaggerated gestures draws the audience's attention away from the points you are trying to make.

- **Don't walk around while telling the joke.**

  Any unnecessary movement distracts the audience and prohibits it from grasping the salient points of your funny story. Any momentary distraction lessens or completely nullifies the laugh.

- **Quote Correctly**

  When you wish to credit a funny line to its originator, quote it *exactly*.

Embellishing the quip doesn't help
it. Comedy professionals strive
to perfect their material. Every line is
written and rewritten, polished and
delivered over and over until it has
just the right rhythm and cadence.
Each word counts. Adding, deleting
or changing a word hurts the quote.

When I interviewed Goodman Ace, the legendary radio and television scribe, for *How the Great Comedy Writers Create Laughter* he pointed out, "You have to put the right word into the right place so the rhythm is there, and the joke makes sense. You can tell a joke to a layman, and he'll repeat it and tell it all wrong. He'll leave out a word or transpose a word."

There is no greater giveaway of a speaker's amateur standing or an indication of the presenter's lack of proper preparation than hearing a famous person misquoted.

Mark Twain once declared from the platform: "Giving up smoking is the easiest thing in the world. I've done it a thousand times."

Here is the same line delivered by a self-impressed, improperly prepared amateur:

"*Mark Twain once said,*
'*I've found through my long years of dealing with tobacco that giving up the terrible habit of smoking without question is the easiest thing in the world to do. You're looking at a man who can say without qualification, I've gone and done it myself a thousand times or more.*'"

Mark Twain never said that. And he's probably turning over in his grave knowing that someone put those bloated words in his mouth.

No self-respecting professional would dare quote the humorist in that manner. It's a breach of integrity and for those who love humor, an unpardonable sin. And what's more the joke loses its impact with those extra words.

Besides, somebody in the audience somewhere, sometime will know when you've misquoted. What's so terrible? Loss of respect. Maybe even loss of future bookings.

I hope these tips for improving technical skills are valuable. They come by years of trial and error. Developing the tools to be an accomplished presenter who uses humor can lead to long-lasting popularity with audiences from the business and professional world as well as social circles.

Anyone who can amuse and entertain others is in great demand for meetings, conferences, conventions, banquets and at a friendly fireside.

When it's laughter you're after no amount of effort is too great. Hearing the audience laugh is sweet music, indeed.

> **"The person who can bring the spirit of laughter into a room is indeed blessed."**
>
> — BENNETT CERF,
> publisher

"If you would rule
the world quietly,
you must
keep it amused."

— RALPH WALDO EMERSON,
poet

Enter The Laughter Zone

"If I can make
people laugh,
then I have served
my purpose for God."

— RED SKELTON,
comedian

Nothing Succeeds Like
a Few Good Laughs

L

LAUGH LONG AND LOUD. A robust rib-rattler improves not only your mood, but also your health. The physical act of laughing helps you stay alert, makes it easier to cope and lets you maintain your sanity when the world gets a little crazy.

A

ADMIT YOU'RE HUMAN (it's true, isn't it?) and laugh at yourself. People who have mastered Living 101 take their work seriously, but not themselves. Knowing the difference gives you the keys to the kingdom.

U

UP YOUR LAUGH QUOTIENT. Nothing may be more important to your health and happiness. The average American laughs 15 times daily. So eat your broccoli and get a megadose of **Vitamin L** every day.

G

GENERATE MIRTH wherever you go. Good humor is the best business and social lubricant. It smoothes understanding, communication and cooperation. Make it your mission to elicit as many smiles as you can each day.

H

HELP YOURSELF SUCCEED without stressing out. Humor is nature's antidote for tension. Let it be your secret weapon when you're up to your eyeballs in alligators. It's fast, it's fun, it's free. No other stress buster can make this claim!

T

TAKE YOUR FUNNY BONE TO WORK. Instigate laughter on the job. Treating co-workers with respect and a sense of mirth does miracles for teamwork and trust.

E

EMBRACE THE NOTION that humor is NOT incompatible with dignity and stature. Humor is the hole that lets the hot air out of a stuffed shirt. Follow the lead of Lincoln, Reagan and JFK who knew that humor is vital in overcoming adversity.

R

REMEMBER THAT LAUGHTER and longevity go hand in hand. Grumps don't live longer — it just seems like it. A buoyant outlook may be more important than oat bran and pushups, and it's easier to take. So get in the zone:
Love life, laugh a lot, last longer.

Your Own Humor Library

A smile
is the cheapest
way to improve
your looks,
even if your teeth
are crooked.

*If you can't
remember a joke;
don't dismember it.*

Your Own Humor Library:
First Aid For The Psyche

THOSE OF US WHO ARE IN THE HUMOR business need a constant supply of funny quotations, anecdotes and stories at our finger tips. But one needn't have professional motives for assembling a good humor repertoire. A collection of amusing materials can be a great source of pleasure for anyone with a funny bone.

Start by keeping an eye out for things that are funny. Observe cartoons, greeting cards, business memos.

I'm always on the lookout for new stories from friends, newspapers, magazines, newsletters, radio, TV, and wherever I can hear them.

Over the years I've collected nearly 1,000 volumes of jokes — everything from *Joe Miller's*

240

Jestbook printed in 1739 to *Milton Berle's Private Joke File.*

I've compiled another 100,000 jokes and stories neatly typed and housed in looseleaf notebooks on my office shelves. They are alphabeticaly catagorized from Aardvarks to Zucchini. All in all, 25,000 jokes, quips, and funny stories have been published in my 53 books.

There are literally thousands of funny stories on every conceivable subject. There's no reason to ever be without a good inventory. Here is some suggested reading to get you started:

Your Own Humor Library:
Dickson, Paul. Jokes. New York: Delacorte Press. 1984.
McKenzie, E.C. 14,000 Quips & Quotes. New York.
    Arlington House, Inc. 1984.
Rosten, Leo. Giant Book of Laughter. New York:
    Crown Publishers, Inc. 1985.

Step One
Armour, Richard. Light Armour. New York:
    McGraw-Hill. 1968.
Armour, Richard. Out of My Mind. New York:
    McGraw-Hill. 1972.
Lebowitz, Fran. Social Studies. New York:
    Random House. 1981
Nash, Ogden. Pocket Book of Ogden Nash. New York:
    Pocket Books. 1962.
Nash, Ogden. Marriage Lines. New York: Pocket
    Books. 1965.
Thurber, James. 92 Stories. New York: Avenel Books. 1990.
Robertson, Jeanne. Humor The Magic of Genie.
    Houston: Rich Publishing Co. 1990.

Step Two
Cousins, Norman. Anatomy of an Illness. New York:
    Norton, 1979.
Kushner, H. When All You've Ever Wanted Isn't Enough: The
    Search for Life That Matters. New York: Summit, 1986.

Mindess, Harvey, et al. Antioch Humor Test:
    Making Sense of Humor: Avon, 1985.
Moody, Raymond A, Jr. Laugh After Laugh: The Healing Power
    of Humor. Jacksonville, FL: Headwaters Press, 1978.

Step Three

Griffith, Joe. Speaker's Library of Business Stories, Anecdotes
    and Humor. Englewood Cliffs: Prentice-Hall, 1990.
Hay, Peter. Book of Business Anecdotes, The.
    New York: Facts On File, 1988.
Iapoce, Michael. A Funny Thing Happened on the Way to the
    Boardroom. New York: John Wiley & Sons, 1988.
Kushner, Malcolm. The Light Touch. How to Use Humor For
    Business Success. New York: Simon and Schuster. 1990.
Perret, Gene. Funny Business. Englewood Cliffs:
    Prentice Hall. 1990.

Step Four

Blakely, James "Doc". Handbook of Wit & Pungent Humor.
    Houston: Rich Publishing, 1980.
Blakely, James "Doc". Push Button Wit. Houston: Rich
    Publishing, 1986.
Klein, Allen. The Healing Power of Humor. Los Angeles:
    Jeremy P. Tarcher, Inc., 1989.
Klein, Allen. Quotations to Cheer You Up When the World Is
    Getting You Down. New York: Sterling Publishing Co. Inc.
    1991.
Metcalf, C.W. and Roma Felible. Lighten Up: Reading, MA:
    Addison-Wesley Publishing Company, 1992.
McManus, Ed & Bill Nichols. We're Roasting Harry Tuesday
    Night. Englewood Cliffs: Prentice-Hall, 1984.

Funny Times
A Monthly Newspaper of Humor, Politics and Fun
P.O. Box 18530 Cleveland, Hts. OH 44118 (216) 371-8600

Journal of Nursing Jocularity, The Humor Magazine for Nurses
P.O. Box 40416 Mesa, AZ 85274
(602) 835-6165

Laughter Works Newsletter
Box 1076   Fair Oaks, CA 95628   (916) 863-1592
Jim Pelley

Step Five
Blumenfeld, Esther & Lynne Alpern. The Smile Connection.
New York: Prentice-Hall Press, 1986.
Buxman, Karyn & Anne LeMoine. Nursing Perspectives on
Humor. Staten Island: Power Publications, 1995.
Peter, Laurence J., and Bill Dana. The Laughter
Prescription. New York: Ballantine, 1982.

Humor 101
Eastman, Max. Enjoyment of Laughter. New York:
Simon and Schuster. 1936.
Freud, Sigmund. Jokes and Their Relation to the
Unconscious. New York: W.W. Norton & Co. 1960
Rapp, Albert. The Origins of Wit and Humor. New
York: E.P. Dutton & Co. Inc. 1951.

When It's Laughter Your After
Allen, Steve. How To Be Funny. Steve Allen with Jane
Wollman. New York: McGraw Hill, 1987.
Antion, Tom. Wake 'Em Up: How to Use Humor and Other
Professional Techniques to Create Alarmingly Good
Business Presentations. Landover Hills, MD: Anchor
Publishing. 1997.
Kushner, Malcolm. Successful Presentations For
Dummies. Chicago: IDG Books Worldwide, 1996
Paulson, Terry. Making Humor Work. Los Altos, CA:
Crisp 1989.
Perret, Gene. How to Hold Your Audience With Humor
Cincinnati: Writer's Digest Books, 1984.
Walters, Lilly. What To Say When You're Dying On The
Platform. New York: McGraw-Hill, Inc. 1995.

Presentation Humor Services
Executive Speaker, The
P.O. Box 292437 Dayton, Ohio 45429
Robert O. Skovgard Editor & Publisher (937) 294-8493

Executive Speechwriter Newsletter, The
Words, Ink Emerson Falls Business Park
St. Johnsbury, Vermont 05819 (802) 748-4472

Jokesmith, The 44 Queens View Road, Marlborough, MA 01752
Ed McManus (508) 481-0979

HUMOR OATH

I do solemnly (and with a semi-straight face)
swear to <u>love, honor</u> & <u>nurture</u> my
SENSE OF HUMOR

I promise to SMILE for no reason
whatsoever, and to enjoy <u>at least</u>
15 BELLY LAUGHS a day.

I believe that CHEERFULNESS is highly
contagious and I will spread JOY to everyone
I meet, including <u>total strangers</u>.

I believe that a PLAYFUL SPIRIT
cures terminal tightness,
cerebral stiffness & hardening
of the attitudes.

Therefore I shall encourage
unrestrained LEVITY in my family,
friends & colleagues.

From this day forward, I promise
to LAUGH more often,
LIVE more lightly, &
fall hopelessly in LOVE with
the sunny side of life.

About the Author

The Larry Wilde "Humor Library" — consisting of 53 books — has sold more than 12 million copies. It is the largest-selling joke book series in publishing history. *The New York Times* has acclaimed Larry "America's Best-Selling Humorist."

Wilde has been making people laugh for over forty years. As a stand-up comedian he shared the bill with many top performers in major nightclubs and Las Vegas showrooms.

He appeared on dozens of TV programs including *The Tonight Show* and *The Mary Tyler Moore Show*, movies and commercials.

His hardcover books *The Great Comedians Talk About Comedy* and *How The Great Comedy Writers Create Laughter* were published to wide acclaim. His funny quips and stories often appear in *Reader's Digest*.

A recognized authority on humor, Wilde is a keynote speaker, seminar leader, and consultant for corporations, associations, and healthcare professionals. He presents programs on how successful people use humor to alleviate stress, promote wellness and achieve personal fulfillment.

In 1976 he founded *National Humor Month* to heighten public awareness of the positive, therapeutic value of laughter. It begins each year on April Fools' Day.

Wilde is also founder and director of *The Carmel Institute of Humor*, fostering research and discussion on the significant role humor plays in wellness, longevity and improved human relations.

Larry lives on the central California coast with his wife, author Maryruth Wilde.

Let's Hear
From You

If you'd like to receive more information on programs, audiotapes and other materials, or you'd like to share how a sense of humor has helped you overcome your alligators, I'd very much enjoy hearing from you.

A sequel to this book is already in the works. If your experience is included in the new "Alligators," you will receive a complimentary copy.

Write me
c/o Jester Press
25470 Cañada Drive
Carmel, CA 93923-8926